Going Beyond

Going Beyond

A Christian Response to Challenges

Kathy Hoppe

Beyondbelief.life Copyright © 2020 Kathy Hoppe
All rights reserved.
ISBN-13: 9798635709061

DEDICATION

I think of all who have travelled before me or who are near the end of their journey. I don't know when or where my travels will cease but I hope I can live as fully as these people.

This book is dedicated to my friends and family who go before me. To my dad, Henry Laverne "Buddy" King who taught me how to think. And to my mom who is still living, Audrey Marie Brackeen King, who always told me I was special and anything is possible.

CONTENTS

Going beyond   1

Beyond panic.   5

Beyond fear   14

Beyond attack   21

Beyond social isolation   28

Beyond sinking   35

Beyond neediness   40

Beyond lonely   44

Beyond nothingness   47

Beyond me   52

Beyond my need   57

Beyond appearances   61

Beyond the center   65

Beyond hurt   69

Beyond regret   73

Beyond sadness   76

Beyond success   81

Beyond anxiety   86

Beyond the black box   91

Beyond rumors   96

Beyond stuck   103

Beyond bad news   107

Beyond harmful words   113

Beyond fairy tales   119

Beyond bitterness   123

Beyond disunity   127

Beyond balance   134

Beyond identity   139

Beyond Easter   146

Bibliography   153

About the author   161

Endnotes   163

GOING BEYOND

The only way to discover the limits of the possible is to go beyond them to the impossible.

Arthur C. Clarke

Where to begin? How in the world did we end up facing our current circumstances? Never in our lives have we faced a situation such as this. It's disrupting our lives and will have long-lasting effects on all of us. You know what your life looked like before this crisis. You thought you knew where it was going. Now you live in uncertainty. But is this a new place? Or does it represent a place you've been before?

Many times, we become lost in the middle of the journey because life doesn't follow a straight path. There are lots of twists, curves, mountains, and ruts along the way. Sometimes we lose our footing. Other times we're rolling down the hill, laughing as we go. Yet in some moments, we are stuck in the pothole. And then we're in the between here and there. In the rut, we only see what's immediately around us. In the forest, we see the trees. When a river rises before us, we wonder how we will cross.

It's hard to see beyond the present circumstances to where we need to go or where we want to be. Someone once said, "Don't limit your challenges. Challenge your limits." Most of us settle for only what's directly in front of us or what is simple to achieve.

But why do we stop there when we could go beyond that? What if, like Indiana Jones in The Last Crusade, we step out of a ledge onto the nonexistent bridge? Might we fall into the chasm to our untimely demise or, perhaps, we will find that which we are seeking? Which direction shall we choose?

This book explores where you are now: living in panic and fear, attacked by something you cannot control, socially distancing to protect yourself and others, and keep your head above water so you don't sink. During this time, you can't help but face yourself, your identity and relationships. Self-examination can lead to despair or growth. The lessons can lead you to a deeper experience in life if you're willing to go beyond this present dilemma.

The premise of this book is based upon the image of concentric circles. Your primary concern is yourself and that's how it should be. Beyond that, you worry about your family. Moving outward, your loyalty is to your friends. As you move towards the edges, you face other people, groups, your community, country, and world, all of whom are facing this catastrophe as well.

Times like these are a chance to reconsider what you believe and practice: about yourself, family, friends, peers, social connections, and all other people. As you do so, things will bubble to the surface: your fears, need for connection and independence, for success, and the future. You'll remember times of pain and sadness. At times you will feel trapped or stuck. You may face bad news such as illness, death, or other losses. But you may also learn new ways to relate to yourself and others.

The call of this work is to go beyond. Don't settle for what's comfortable. Don't stay in your current state. Go beyond that and place yourself in uncomfortable spots with people you don't know, even in your social isolation and while protecting yourself, or in situations that require an emotional or situational risk, calling you to do something different or relate to people in new ways. Go beyond your present panic. Go beyond your future fears. Consider this an invitation to become an adventurer. Pack up your motivation, strength, and desire and follow me into the land beyond belief.

Reflection

1. Think about your life before this crisis. Were you truly satisfied?
2. In what ways are you dissatisfied? Are there goals you desire but have not moved toward? What can you do to make movement on those?
3. Think of someone you most admire. What qualities do they have? What prevents you from having those?

_____

_____

_____

_____

_____

_____

_____

BEYOND PANIC

In my experience, the words "now just calm down" almost inevitably have the opposite effect on the person you are speaking to.

Elyn R. Saks

We are facing an unprecedented moment. The pandemic situation is changing rapidly and it's difficult to stay on top of it. It's like the beachball that refuses to submerge. Every time we try to grab it, control it, or get on it, it slips away.

How in the world did we get here? Pandemics aren't new. There are centuries of pandemic history dating back to the 2nd century starting with the Antonine plague. The death toll was 5 million people. Wide-spread illness continued and in the 14th century, humans faced the worst – the Black Death (Bubonic plague) which killed 200 million people. That was followed by smallpox in the 16thcentury, the Great Plagues in the 16th & 17th century, and then cholera, yellow fever, the Russian flu, and then in the early 20th century, the Spanish flu taking 40-50 million lives. In my lifetime, we've faced HIV/AIDS, the Asian flu, the Hong Kong flu, the Swine flu, SARS, MERS, and Ebola.[1]

About 15 years ago, I attended a day long workshop on community preparation for pandemic crisis. We were informed then that a worldwide pandemic was coming. We just didn't know when or how it would occur.

Others also saw it coming and began to plan ahead. The World Health Organization developed a rapid response protocol. Homeland Security and the US developed a national strategy for pandemic influenza. Now is the time for those. We have more tools than ever before including technology, multiple forms of communication, and rapid implementation.

The greatest challenge we face is public cooperation. When people do not understand the importance and timeliness of social isolation, they become part of the problem. For the rest of us, our biggest enemy is not the emergency. It is our own fear and panic. That's what we need to discuss. When an event initially occurs, we tend to be complacent and take little notice. We knew there was a problem in December 2019. But it was another country's issue, not ours. It took a while to get our attention.

Now we face insufficient or changing information. This is a new strain. While it is part of the coronavirus, we do not yet know all of its limits. We do know that it is highly contagious, spreads easily, and can become severe, even leading to death. We are learning "on the go." Because of that, we feel like everything is out of control. There is no "normal" anymore. We all feel a loss of control.

That loss of control, coupled with constantly changing information, makes us fearful of many things. It means that we have changing work demands and reduced social capacity.

We need to be in this for the long haul. It may not end in a few weeks. More likely, we are looking at several months. Because of that, we will all experience decreasing stamina.

For those of us who are believers, we know the Bible talks about these things. Jesus words remind us that we will face great trials. "Nation will fight nation and ruler fight ruler, over and over. Huge earthquakes will occur in various places. There will be famines. You'll think at times that the very sky is falling!" (Luke 21:10–11). Kind of feels like that, doesn't it? It takes all of us!

So, how will we get through this? It will take all of us. There are things you need to do personally. Some are things that leaders need to do for us. Our organizations need to pitch as well. Together, as a community, we will endure the current hardship. And one year, two years, five years from now, we will remember this time as difficult but will also remember how we came together in community to overcome the difficulties.

How can you personally help with the poor information? First, make sure that you are getting accurate information. There are rumors, myths, and all kinds of news that is not helpful. Don't rely on your neighbor, or social media, or other sources for good information. Find your information from trustworthy source.

Become a myth-buster! Whenever you hear someone say, "Oh, young people don't get this." Bust the myth. Everyone can get this virus. If someone says, "Everyone who gets it will die." Bust the myth. More people will recover from this than will die. The symptoms are very uncomfortable.

Finally, limit yourself to information to twice daily. When someone listens to information all day, it increases their panic and fear. That's when we make bad decisions. I remember working in a place when Katrina hit and having the news station on all day long. I looked at my co-workers and said, "We need to change the channel. This is not helping. And, in some cases, it is traumatizing people." You can get the information from twice daily briefings.

How can you deal with the loss of control? Two things mainly. Focus on what you can control. You can control your reactions and responses. You can still control how you think and what you say. Give other people options. Remember, they're experiencing a loss of control. Ask, "Would you like to talk now or later?" "Would you like water or tea?" Remember, giving one another options returns a sense of control.

The other thing to remember is that we really never had control over our lives. We had the illusion of control. Think of all the times when something unexpected has happened. We have all faced deaths, separations, job losses, income loss, unexpected bills, illnesses. We didn't have control of which or when any of those happened to us. The best thing we can do is accept our loss of control.

I'm reminded of an illustration someone once told me. When sailing on a boat, the best sailors develop "sea legs." That's the ability to move with boat as it rocks. We need to practice that now. That requires adaptability and flexibility. Don't forget to use your sea legs!

Think about all the fears we face. Our biggest fear is of the unknown. We're not certain what we're facing, or how long it will be present. We don't know how long we will need to practice social isolation. We don't know what the immediate future holds.

We fear getting ill. What if I get sick? Will it be serious? Will I infect others? We fear death. What if I die? We fear people. What if they're sick? What if they touch me? What if I touch something and it's infected? We fear isolation. How can I live without my friends? What if I don't get to see parts of my family again? We fear exclusivity or stigmatism. What if people label me if I get sick? What if people find out I'm helping someone who's sick? How will they treat me? We fear jobs – the loss of jobs, being demoted, being laid off, and the loss of income. All of these are realistic fears. So, how can you handle those fears? First, acknowledge them aloud to yourself. Don't let them rattle around your head.

Next, talk about your fears with someone who can support you. You don't need false promises. You need someone who will really listen and let you know they hear you.

Face your fears. Ask yourself what's the worst thing that can happen? Is it likely? Ask what will happen next. Is that probable? Take it all the way down the line. Look for how it becomes illogical and unlikely. You are so much stronger than you know. You have survived many things in life. You will survive this as well.

Think about the changes in work. We've all had a change in schedule. Some are working more; some are working less. Some have changed locations or are working in unfamiliar areas. Some of us have changing roles every day. The demands on us have changed. Maybe it's longer hours or more weekends with fewer breaks.

We've had a change in exposure to risk. And the people around us have changed. How can we deal with this? Most importantly, remember, this is temporary. It will not last. Now it may last more than a few weeks, or a few months, but it will end.

A story someone once told me helps me. We are all going through a tunnel and it feels very dark right now. But it's a tunnel. That means we will reach the end and will step once again into the light.

Because of all the changes, our social lives have altered. We're not able to meet friends for dinner, or have parties, or go to sporting events. Yet, connection is vital. We have to find ways to stay connected.

Engage people you do see. I'm practicing what I call leaning away while leaning in. I stay 6' away or wear personal protective equipment but I'm leaning in emotionally. I'm still looking at you, hearing you, and being empathic while keeping a safe physical distance.
Engage people by acknowledging them. They're afraid and they're stressed. They need you to understand that. They may not know how to say that.

Use technology to connect. Use your phone, social media, or other platforms. I attend church via computer. I meet with my community group in an online meeting space. I talk with my family on the phone frequently.

Schedule time to connect. Don't let your help overtake your need for connection. Listen for the stories of hope.

Hang in there! You are going to experience decreasing stamina. That's why it's so important for you to scan your body and your mind. We're running a marathon, not a sprint.

Years ago, I trained for a marathon. I didn't try to run far at first. I ran 1", the next day I ran 2", then 3, and so on. By the end of 3 months, I could for 60". Then I began doing longer runs. Finally, I ran 26.2 miles. I paced myself. I stopped when I need to. I took care of my basic needs. I finished the race. Remember, the race prize goes to those who keep on running, not to those who finish first.

Get plenty of rest. Practice some mindfulness techniques and be self-compassionate. Focus on your "why." Remember what you're called to do and be. That will keep you going strong.

Leaders, provide your staff, your volunteers, or your people with information. Ensure it's accurate and up to date. Be patient with their questions. Encourage their input.

Protect your staff. Support and monitor their physical and emotional well-being. Step in when you need to and let them take a break or a day off.

Encourage the use of a buddy system. Have them find someone

else with whom they work and trust. Tell them to step in when one is not feeling well, or not responding well. If they give one another permission to do that, then they're more likely to seek help when they need it.

Offer team meetings or debriefing times frequently. These can be done via technology. Let people share their struggles but remind them to share positive stories. Be the island of peace in the sea of chaos. Stay calm and focus on hope.

To everyone, remember God's words to Joshua who faced the unknown, the giants in the land, who worked with a rebellious tribe, and who was uncertain of himself. "Be strong and courageous. Do not fear or be in dread, for it is the Lord your God who goes with you. He will not leave you or forsake you" (Deuteronomy 31:6).

And don't forget to look around for all the miracles! They're all around you. I see miracles like expanding creativity, acts of kindness, people reaching out, giving more than ever before. Move beyond panic - be contagious with good news.

Reflection

1. How is God showing you to move beyond your panic?

2. What things prevent your panic from growing?

3. How can you support others who experience panic?

BEYOND FEAR

Don't give in to your fears.
If you do, you won't be able to talk to your heart.

Paulo Coelho

What if? These are powerful words.

Choose wisely. I can still picture the scene: Indiana Jones, a hat-wearing, adventure-seeking archeologist forever in search of the truth learned from artifacts, and now on the trail in search of the Holy Grail, finds himself in the presence of the Grail Knight. While it may seem simple, the professor is faced with choosing the correct chalice among at least fifty golden ones sparkling in the cave candlelight. Rushing forward, the crusader hesitates when the Grail Knight speaks, "Choose wisely, for while the true Grail will bring you life, the false Grail will take it from you." Drinking the cup can bring everlasting freedom from all life's difficulties with a renewed mind and body or poison one. I can hear him thinking . . . "What if I choose the wrong one and my father dies?" "What if I choose the right one and I drink it myself?" "What if…"

What if the world of the corona virus frenzy we are living out with news changing by the hour changes the world as I know it? What if I cancel this event? What if I go to church? What if the schools shut down? What if I get sick and am quarantined and have no vacation or sick leave? What if I lose business? What if I lose my job? What if this spreads further? What if someone else dies? What if I get on that plane, boat, in that car, go somewhere else? What if I'm trapped in my house without basics, like toilet paper? What if goes a thousand directions in the land of fear.

What if defines my life many times. What if I write a blog and no one reads it? What if I write a book and no one buys it? What if I plan a retreat and no one comes? What if I spend too much, too little, or buy the wrong things? What if no one likes me? What if someone does but I don't want them to like me? What if I run out of money, time, resources, energy? What ifs run around in my head like a pack of mice nibbling wherever they find residence in my brain as if it's made of cheese. Sometimes my head hurts from all the fear.

"Don't be afraid," you say. Ok, well let's get really honest. That DOES NOT help me! You might as well watch me eat rat poison and tell me I will be fine. I want to shout, "Ok, let's see how you do this. I declare your salary is cut by $20,000 from this point forward." How are you feeling now? Don't worry.

Or how about this one? A very close relative has a few weeks to live but don't be afraid. What? Ok, try this one on – you've just been told your child will die within a week. Still want me to tell you not to be afraid?

In the nitty gritty of life, when the heart is pounding, and the alarm system of the brain is going nuts, sending endocrine alarms throughout your body, that last part of your system that's actually working well is your logic. This wonderful creation of God is designed to go on high alert and get you out of the lion's den when you're thrown in the midst of a pride of hungry cubs. Your autonomic system will respond, ready to fight, flee, or freeze. Your thinking skills will decrease. But don't be afraid.

Let's stop telling people how to think or feel and start helping them find their way through these times of desperation. We have a great example from the widow of Zarephath in 1 Kings. God tells Elijah to go to this town and find the WIDOW WITH NO NAME whom God has commanded to hide and feed him. When Elijah finds her, he must notice her fright because he says, "Don't be afraid."

Let's picture this. The hometown girl made big and nasty, Jezebel, married to the current and abhorrent King Ahab, has a #1 enemy, namely Elijah, who dares to speak doom and gloom, and, by the way, arises out of nowhere, is a nobody, and hasn't yet the claim to fame for any miraculous event, shows up at your well, on the run and asks you for food and drink. You're on your last leg, dirt poor, no more food, drought all around, and your desperation is so great, you know you and your beloved son have one meal left, and then it's all downhill from there. You don't have any favor because you're a widow, ignored by the locals, the writer of this story who refuses to name you, and the scholars and preachers who skip over you to focus on the great prophet, Elijah. And you're told, "Don't be afraid!" Really?! Well, now, that helps, right? Or does it?

The WIDOW WITH NO NAME acquiesces and provides bread and water for the prophet for perhaps three years. I can see how this WIDOW WITH NO NAME decides to obey, and because there always seems to be one more meal that miraculously appears each day, becomes hospitable. Maybe this daily renewal supply convinces the WIDOW WITH NO NAME that all will be okay. And it's livable, like most of us will experience over the next few months in our quarantined state of existence. Not preferable, but alive. Until…her son dies. And the WIDOW WITH NO NAME is furious!

I can't say I blame her. After all, if I trusted you, O powerful prophet of God, Elijah, and I obeyed God and gave up my food, drink, and space, with a threat on your life, and by extension, my own and my son's life, then I would be pretty ticked when my son dies anyway. I sacrificed A WHOLE LOT to keep you safe, warm, and fed. Some thanks I get. And you're the one who told me, "Don't be afraid!"

Once upon a time I was pregnant with a beautiful baby boy. I worked for an international adoption agency at the time and made a not well-timed and flippant remark about how I thought it was good that people had a waiting period for adoption then because a pregnant woman has to wait nine months. (I know, there I go sticking my foot in my mouth again and being thoughtless – I really do feel bad about that now). One of the case workers, who had adopted some children, said, "At least you know where your child is, and it's safe." Oops. I think she felt kind of bad 5 months later when my baby died. Both of us were wrong. Rather than supporting one another, we were saying, "Don't be afraid," but not with the best of hearts.

So, the WIDOW WITH NO NAME is distraught with grief. I've heard some say that God brings us suffering to remind us of our need for him. STOP IT! That's not bringing her close to God. I didn't need my baby to die for me to get nearer to the Holy One. My loved one doesn't need cancer to remind him of his depravity – it ain't working. What does the WIDOW WITH NO NAME need? Think of all she has given up to keep this prophet safe. We think the story is about him. I suppose that's part of it. But, isn't the story about her? Elijah does good. He does the right thing. He begs God for her son's life, and we see the first resurrection in the Bible in this passage as her son comes back to life. How does the WIDOW WITH NO NAME respond? She doesn't say, "I'm not afraid." She doesn't say, "I believe in God now. My faith was poor before." Instead, she says, "Now I know you are a man of God and that the word of the Lord from your mouth is the truth" (v. 24). Hmm. The proof is in the pudding, or so my mom used to say. The WIDOW WITH NO NAME can trust Elijah because his actions match his words. Do your deeds or gifts to others convince them that your words of faith are real?

In our community group, we decided this woman should no longer be ignored by us, the prophet, the preachers, or the scholars, or anyone else. So, we decided to name her Hope. She demonstrated hope every morning when she arose to make bread from non-existent ingredients. Her portrayal of hope in the midst of harboring a fugitive is remarkable. She speaks of her desire for hope when she expresses her disappointment and anger at the prophet and his lack of fulfillment of an unspoken contract of mutual protection. Her practice of hope is evident in her belief that in the midst of a desperate situation, and her beliefs that life is over, she finds purpose and meaning in her life – protecting, providing, and promoting God's chosen one.

Here's the other side of the question. What if God doesn't "cause" suffering so we can know how bad we are, and how good He is? What if God shows us in the midst of pain, some brought by a fallen world, and some we bring upon ourselves through our sinful desires and irrational thoughts that we cannot live without toilet paper and baby wipes and hand sanitizer, what if we see our meaning and purpose in life more clearly? What if, like HOPE, the WIDOW WITH NO NAME, we become extravagant givers to those around us, offering connection despite isolation, hope instead of despair, and a place of peace & safety in the sea of chaos? What if we moved beyond fear?

Choose wisely. Like the Holy Grail, my response to fear can speak volumes to those around me. Can I find meaning and purpose? Do the "what ifs" lead me to reach out and beyond my fear to those who are in need? Which cup of "what ifs" am I drinking from? The "what if" everything goes wrong or the "what if" some marvelous miracle happens? One will poison me; the other will give me life. Come with me. Let's move beyond fear.

Reflection

1. Think about your fears. What do you fear most? Is it likely to happen?

2. Remember a time in the past when you faced something dreadful? What happened? What do you need to move beyond your fears?

_____

_____

_____

_____

_____

_____

_____

_____

_____

_____

BEYOND ATTACK

Famous survivors of the Spanish Flu of 1918: Walt Disney, Edvard Munch, Woodrow Wilson, FDR, Georgia O'Keefe, Mary Pickford, Mahatma Gandhi, Amelia Earhart, T. S. Eliot, Igor Stravinsky, John Steinbeck, D.H. Lawrence.

Feeling under attack? Some are calling it the zombie apocalypse. Others are devising names to call this thing – this assault on all of us. It's interfering with our lives, our families, our work, and our plans. Think of all the ways in which your life has changed in the past weeks.

Baby showers – postponed. Family visits – cancelled. Classes – moved to online. Continuing education – postponed. Work – moved to remote. Counseling sessions – moved to teletherapy. Just in Oklahoma alone the following occurred: in one week 3 confirmed cases, Monday – 10, Tuesday – 17, and today at noon –

29. And the count goes even higher.

And the uncertainty of how long this will last zips around the room like a pesky fly. Just when it lands and you think you can capture the irritable pest, it changes directions and flits off to another jetty out of reach. It refuses to stay in one place long enough for you to gain a sense of mastery.

Life is out of our control at this moment. It feels odd, doesn't it? But we are not strangers to unpredictability. The problem is that our complacency led us to believe that we had control over anything. We never did.

If you live long enough, you gain a sense of this. Ambiguity has shadowed us throughout life. I was a young child in the late 1950s when school desegregation was implemented, and we wondered what would happen next. Then Buddy Holly died, and we thought the music died with him – but it didn't.

We didn't have a Civil Rights Act until 1960, and that took a lot of protest. Then the first Catholic was appointed president. What? How could that possibly work? That was followed by the Bay of Pigs fiasco and hiding under our desks because of the nuclear threat. I remember being in the first grade when President Kennedy was assassinated. The country was gripped with fear.

Then we had Vietnam, that horrible, no-nonsense conflict that caused so much harm to so many Americans and non-Americans. We endured Desert Storm, the OKC bombing, Katrina, 9-11, terrorist acts, and devastating tornadoes. So many disasters, too many to name. In 2012 alone, I lived through a hurricane, earthquake, and flood all within one month.

This doesn't even count the personal tragedies each of us suffered during all these times. Loss of children, parents, siblings, spouse. Being laid off repeatedly, finding new jobs, moving to different places, and always looking for that situation where the indeterminate sleuth of question was banished. When would we find a spot that was calm, peaceful, and full of promise?

Yet we did have those moments, didn't we? Joyous celebrations of weddings, babies, job promotions, better things that came our way along with new opportunities and increasing friends. Those are the times we choose to remember, some occurring naturally, others catching us by surprise, and all as gifts from the good Lord. We treasure those, don't we?

We forget that we live in world fractured by kingdom rebellion. When Eve & Adam decided they could be like God, the system shifted. Think of the butterfly effect. One slight movement in the wrong direction, and from that point forward, the consequences proved devastating. They were clearly warned but their desire to have and be equals with God compromised their life of luxury and ease.

And we are born into that space, the in-between of paradise and not yet. We live our lives in the middle of vagueness, fooled into thinking we understand ourselves and everything around us, that we deserve only the best, and certainly the promise of good health and fortune. That existence lulls us into a sleeping beauty trance and life seems like a fairy tale. But it isn't. Soon enough, a tragedy occurs.

During these times of disruption, we have opportunities. Do we choose to complain of inconvenience, or do we practice gratitude for the present comforts we do have? Do we gripe about other people or offer thanks to those who have given so much of their time, resources, and energy to create a better world? Do we seek to rely on our craft and skill or is our reliance upon the one who is Holy and who has always been with us?

The Psalmist declares, "The Lord is my rock, my fortress and my deliverer; my God is my rock, in whom I take refuge, my shield and the horn of my salvation, my stronghold" (Ps. 18:2). While that's a proclamation of who God is, it's also a recognition of who I am and a prediction of what is yet to come.

Hard times bring us to analysis. We can use our reflection to criticize others or we can use it to examine ourselves, our lives, and things that we hold dear. Do those need to change? Only you and God can answer that. Do I need to be more kind, more giving, gentler, or more intentional? Do I need more of God and less of me?

And the psalmist alerts us. This thing, this multiplying, life-changing, constantly migrating virus has not completed its journey. We face a dubious future, possibly illness, and with all certainty, economic consequences. While social isolation flattens the curve, and is the right response, it will also produce unforeseeable effects. The danger lies in becoming comfortable with aloneness, and slothfulness in our attunement to others. I have no doubt that mental illness will increase as a result.

We are social beings. While social networking convinces us that our relational needs can be met, it actually has the opposite effect. A 2017 study by researchers at the University of Pennsylvania noted that adults ages 19 – 32 with high social media use were more likely to feel socially isolated.[2] According to The Cigna

Health Insurance Company, loneliness is already an epidemic. Nearly 46% of 20,000 survey respondents expressed loneliness.[3]

Social isolation is also associated with poorer health and higher mortality.[4] Depression, suicidality, and psychosis tend to rise with increased isolation.[5] On the other hand, neighborhoods with high social support and who work together in community alter everyone's perception of stress and buffer against mental illness.[6] It is the connection with one another, face to face, that provides that aid. You see, we have these neural networks that are vital to us. When we are face to face with other humans, our brains have this mirror neuron system that activates. It allows us to experience empathy, love, joy, and the pain of another human being.[7] It's also what helps us to maintain a sense of morality, of rightness and justice. If we cannot relate to one another, then we lose understanding, followed by a sense of moral agency. We neglect one another and ignore the need to protect other beings.

So, am I concerned or worried about the direction we're moving? No. I believe that God will make a way. However, I don't like the unknowingness of it all. That's where the Psalmist brings comfort. He tells me seven ways that God is present and protecting me.

1. God is my rock. This tells me that my feet are on a firm foundation. It may feel like the sands are shifting, but the footing is solid and built on a foundation that will not collapse.

2. God provides a hiding place for me from any enemy that seeks to destroy me. I must draw near and listen to God's whispers of where I need to be at any given moment.

3. God is my fortress. This attack will not prevail. It's a losing battle and the victory in the end will be God's glorious redemption. I don't know when or how that will take place, but I do know that God will not lose.

4. God is also my deliverer, the one who rescues me. I may think I'm in this battle alone, but I have someone who goes before me, above me, below me, and behind me.

5. God is my shield. God stands in front, protecting me from direct assault.

6. God is my savior, my true hero.

7. God is my stronghold. Whenever the storms prevail, and are whipping me about, causing me to think I will surely sink in the ocean of chaos, God is present for me to hold, like the mast on a ship that cannot be broken.

Whenever I'm feeling alone and embattled, I repeat: God is my rock, my fortress, my deliverer, my shield, my savior, and my stronghold. And I turn to my neighbors, and my friends, and support system. I repeat to them: God is your rock, your fortress, your deliverer, your shield, your savior, and your stronghold.

Years ago, I had a dream. In this dream God dropped a rope from the sky and said, "Hang on, and don't let go." Little did I know that vision would protect me from the next catastrophic and life-altering event. I was reminded of that today. And I heard God say again, "Hang on, child, and don't let go."

I think we should hold together. We need to do that. Find ways to connect. Share your fears, challenges, and struggles. Encourage hopes and dreams. Don't always take it seriously. Laugh and love. Together we will move beyond attack.

Reflection

1. How is this current crisis creating change in your beliefs about God?

2. What do you need most from God at this time?

_____

_____

_____

_____

_____

_____

_____

BEYOND SOCIAL ISOLATION

Home is where love resides, memories are created,
friends always belong, and laughter never ends.

Anonymous

How's that working for you – social isolation? This necessary, and yet inconvenient, burrowing down like a prairie dog in winter, though spring has arrived, type of existence is already old. Right? The fun and games, if you had any, over the past few weeks are becoming the things that drive us crazy. Let me borrow examples from my recent clients.

It's wonderful to have so much family time. With public venues closing, families are playing games, doing outside activities, making videos, and eating together. Hooray! They need that and the children are loving it!

Except, wait, wait for it, it's already getting old. Spouses are getting on one another's nerves, and the children's needs and desires for attention never seem fully satisfied. "And if I have to tell my 16-year-old son one more time that he cannot just jump in the car and go wherever he pleases, I'm going to . . . Where is that kid anyway?" Bickering is peeking its little head down our safe, warm tunnels. Boredom is creeping silently around the dark corners. And the news of 6 – 8 more weeks of the togetherness trap is terrifying. And these are all healthy families.

Think of the dysfunctional families – the ones where the spouses are barely enduring one another, on the brink of divorce, some laid off from work with little to no income in the near future, and one or both dealing with substance abuse issues. And the kids – you know the boy with ADHD who is absolutely bouncing off the walls, or perhaps tossing his ball around every surface in the house, knocking things over, constantly interrupting, and "Oh, we forgot to call the doctor for a refill on my medicine!!" Or the teen girl who has totally disappeared in her room, hasn't spoken a word in days, and appears to have an eating disorder since she's constantly exercising, eating very little, and losing a lot of weight. And, oh, dear, the poor people who already have anxiety issues or perhaps OCD. They can't get anything clean enough with the constant news and rising numbers of cases.

Yet others, those who live alone and the elderly, are having a different experience. They may be vicariously experiencing fun as they view the family posts on social media and yet longing for someone with whom they can share a meal. It might be nice to have another body in the room, not just for conversation but for the warm vibes that another human being brings into the environment. Solitude is a big space to hold for oneself.

If people are practicing social distancing, then they are about to experience the unleashing of all their demons. Because now everything they've avoided facing in their relationships, their work, their home, and inner selves are trying to break through the thinning cover of busyness. Most likely, people will find more things to do but the longer the population is confined, the weaker the defenses become. And that can be bad . . . or good.

Reminds me of Jack Nicholas in *The Shining*. It was a luxury resort hotel in a beautiful mountain setting, with a generous salary provided to watch over the place during the down season, and all kinds of hallways to ride a tricycle through. Except . . . well, you know the end of that story.

No matter if family surrounds people, they will experience loneliness. It is a loneliness from the imposed isolation, it's a personal solitude, and it's a universal aloneness. While the first is novel and temporary, the last two are pre-existing and enduring with our over-scheduled lives shielding us from the angst. "The whole conviction of my life now rests upon the belief that loneliness, far from being a rare and curious phenomenon, peculiar to myself and to a few other solitary men, is the central and inevitable fact of human existence."[8]

In his book, *The Bible in 10 Words*, Deron Spoo says, "There are no easy answers to our loneliness. But there are some difficult questions that need to be asked. More than exploring these two questions, we must allow [sic] these two questions to explore us."[9] What an interesting approach! Chase that idea around your cave awhile.

What does it mean to allow something to pursue me? I'm a go-getter, action-oriented, no need to wait, get it done kind of gal. I usually have several projects I'm chasing around the calendar. According to Gallup's StrengthQuest, I'm an achiever. "People exceptionally talented in the Achiever theme work hard and possess a great deal of stamina. They take immense satisfaction in being busy and productive."[10] I am the one who explores things. So, encouraging me to allow awkward questions to explore me is a wee bit uncomfortable.

Deron Spoo's two exploratory questions are: Am I using people to avoid God? And, am I using God to avoid people? Those are worthy questions and I don't want to take away from his insightful book but that's not where I want to lead you. If you desire to hear more of Deron's ideas, I would encourage you to purchase his book, *The Bible in 10 Words*.

My inquiry is a bit different but follows this concept of a question exploring me. With social isolation, loneliness rises. What causes loneliness? Do I feel lonely? My response to the latter is yes. My spouse is still working 10-hour days with a 45" minute drive each way. That means four days a week, I'm alone for 12 hours. Even an overachiever with 20 projects starts feeling the impact of being alone. While I'm an introvert and gain energy from solitude, I need interaction with others. I can count on one hand the number of people who have reached out or called me in the past 3 weeks to check on me. Not that I want anyone to feel bad, because I could pick up the phone and call others. That kind of loneliness is the result of my inaction.

But I felt lonely before the pandemic. How can a person who does so much with so many people and is active in a large church feel so lonely? I'm trying, folks. I'm offering to help, to be involved, to get connected. Back to what causes loneliness. I'm trying to let that question sink in. I say the word aloud, "What is the reason for my loneliness?" That question is rattling in my brain and surging through the neurocircuitry of my whole being. My hands and fingers are tingling, and my stomach is churning, and my legs are itching to run. Hmm. Isn't that curious?

Say it aloud to yourself. "Do I feel lonely?" "What causes my loneliness?" How's that affect you? Remember, Deron's words – allow the question to explore you. If you don't do that, then your logical brain will take over and rationalizations will pop up like conversation balloons in a newspaper cartoon. "Lonely? I'm not lonely." "It's not my fault." "Social isolation – THAT'S the cause of my loneliness!"

When you turn off the prefrontal cortex and let the question bounce around inside your whole being, you probably feel some tenderness, aches, itches, or discomfort in your physical body. What is your body saying to you? When you refrain from answering too quickly and open yourself up to the possibility of your loneliness, you give the Holy Spirit room to get your attention and speak hidden truths.

Here's another perspective. Clark Moustakas says, "Loneliness is not merely a normal part of human life, it is essential for human growth and authentic existence. By truly experiencing loneliness, the individual affirms his being and authenticity. When positively embraced and confronted, loneliness has a salutary role: the integration and deepening of self."[11] Wait just a minute. Think about this. Could loneliness be God's tactic to capture our hearts and speak to our souls?

Seclusion was no stranger to Jesus. One wonders if he was an introvert because he seemed to gain energy from privacy. Yet his calling placed him amid crowds of people. Called into the wilderness, Jesus experiences the temptations of provision, trust, and power. Ooh. The pandemic is threatening our economic stability, testing our belief in governing leaders and one another (as we "work" from homes), and robbing us of control. Sounds a little similar, don't you think?

Yet, in the wilderness Jesus recognizes the tempter and uses scripture against the Evil One. "Jesus said to him, 'Away from me, Satan! For it is written: 'Worship the Lord your God, and serve him only.' Then the devil left him, and angels came and attended him" (Matt. 4:10 – 11). Are you using scripture to fight those demons? Perhaps in the middle of isolation, God is whispering, "I know you. I see your inner core. There are things we need to work on and work through. Are you relying on my provision? Do you trust me? Will you give me control of your life?"

Could it be that you can move beyond loneliness to growth and peace? After all, the flower seed must be buried in the dark and broken apart in order to produce new life. This time may be the healing you need. As you move beyond social isolation, allow all the questions to explore you. See how that changes your life.

Reflection

1. How is God using social distancing to speak to you?

2. What are you learning in this time about yourself and your relationships? What do you need to change once this is over?

BEYOND SINKING

*You find peace not by rearranging the circumstances of your life,
but by realizing who you are at the deepest level.*

Eckhart Tolle

Peace. I am in need of peace—in my mind and heart, in my relationships, in my family. Right now, it seems elusive. Where can one find tranquility in a world that seems out of control, when one cannot control the circumstances surrounding life, loved ones, or even decisions?

Are you at peace? What are the things that prevent you from experiencing a sense of calm and quiet? Is it the current crisis you are facing? The pandemic? Perhaps you've lost a relationship. That hurts so deeply. Or you may have lost your job. That places a lot of pressure on you. Maybe you've just learned some awful news about a loved one's health, or your own. How can you deal with that?

It's so difficult to envision a future when you don't have a present sense of harmony. Your mind is restless and looking for an anchor of some sort, the kind that sinks deep, attaches to bedrock, and keeps your boat steady in the middle of a storm. How is it possible to have peace when your ship is rocking in the storm, threatening to sink you & everyone around?

Remember when Jesus spoke, and the waves quieted? "Late that day he said to them, 'Let's go across to the other side.' They took him in the boat as he was. Other boats came along. A huge storm came up. Waves poured into the boat, threatening to sink it. And Jesus was in the stern, head on a pillow, sleeping! They roused him, saying, 'Teacher, is it nothing to you that we're going down?' Awake now, he told the wind to pipe down and said to the sea, 'Quiet! Settle down!' The wind ran out of breath; the sea became smooth as glass" (Mark 4:35-39).

Picture him now as then. He stands over your life, saying, "Peace, peace. Be still." Just as a boat continues to rock even after the waves have calmed, so will your life. Jesus' words of peace will calm the rising swells of chaos around you. "Still, still." Peace is present, even when you cannot feel it.

Lavender symbolizes peace. Some claim that it makes one feel at ease, relaxed, and so it's recommended for those times when one feels the stress of chaos and disruption (Ansalone, 2015). The plant proves tough in drought, hot sun, dry soil, and even colder temperatures. Its blooms are delicate to the touch (Balogh, 2019). Just like you. God gives you the resources to withstand conditions that may seem harsh, remaining firm during the strongest wind, and yet able to sway in the breeze. Peace will arrive soon, and you can withstand this present moment.

But how do you achieve peace? Wayne Dyer says, "Peace is the result of retraining your mind to process life as it is rather than as you think it should be." Wow, isn't that the truth? So often you want to control how life happens. But sometimes things come your way that you dislike, causing a loss of control.

Do you feel you are drowning? "Being under stress is like being stranded in a body of water. If you panic, it will cause you to flail around so that the water rushes into your lungs and creates further distress. Yet, by calmly collecting yourself and using controlled breath you remain afloat with ease" (Alaric Hutchinson). When sudden events catch us off guard like being laid off, getting sick, receiving an unexpected bill, living through a pandemic, your tendency is to fight it. No matter how well you plan, you will always face uncertainty.

True peace comes only through the Lord. C. S. Lewis reminds us of this, "God cannot give us a happiness and peace apart from Himself, because it is not there. There is no such thing." Isn't that what Paul tells us as well from his jail room in Philippi? "Don't fret or worry. Instead of worrying, pray. Let petitions and praises shape your worries into prayers, letting God know your concerns. Before you know it, a sense of God's wholeness, everything coming together for good, will come and settle you down. It's wonderful what happens when Christ displaces worry at the center of your life" (Phil. 4:6-7).

The thing you fail to recognize is that you never had control. You had the illusion of control. You can no more control your life than the queen ant can protect her hive when you step on it. What you can control, though, is how you respond to situations. Ghandi said, "Each one has to find his peace from within. And peace to be real must be unaffected by outside circumstances."

In John 14:27, Jesus reminds us that he leaves his peace with us. And that is the peace that is deep and found only in close relationship with him. The more time you spend on your knees in prayer, the closer you grow to Christ, and the more you find your calm in him.

Remember these two lessons: you are not alone, peace will arrive soon, and you can withstand this present moment. Today move beyond sinking. Learn to stay afloat.

Reflection

1. What prevents you from having peace?

2. How can you change within to bring a sense of peace?

3. How can prayer bring a sense of calm and tranquility?

BEYOND NEEDINESS

Trust yourself.
Create the kind of self that you will be happy to live with all your life.
Make the most of yourself by fanning the tiny,
 inner sparks of possibility into flames of achievement.

Golda Meir

Meeting with my co-workers at lunch one day, we were discussing what we might do if something happened to our spouses. I joked about having a contingency plan when I was younger. Indeed, I had a plan B. I had chosen someone to marry me because he was employed, responsible, and would make a good father. I wasn't interested in a relationship with him, just a safety net. Of course, he never knew of this plan. When years later, I shared this plan with my spouse, he simply laughed. My kids grew up and the plan was unnecessary. But lately I've been thinking what if something happens to my spouse now? How will I make it? Perhaps I need a new action plan, just in case. But as we laughed about this at lunch, I realized I don't "need" someone else. I am well-supplied and self-sufficient. I can take care of myself.

While I speak in other places about moving beyond myself and beyond independence, and while I still believe that we need one another as human beings, I am not incomplete without someone else. This is so important to realize. And it speaks to my own growth through the years to realize that I am complete. I was created by the Holy One, and with God's love and support, I am whole. But I've not always thought or felt this way.

Years ago I couldn't imagine a life without someone special to love me. I was distraught in high school when no one asked me out for dates during my senior year. I initially found someone in college for the first year but then spent the remaining years of university life without a solid, steady boyfriend. I even went a full two years without dating anyone. I was feeling desperate. Other people told me I was too independent, I wasn't submissive enough, I was too bossy, too smart, too religious, so on and so forth. As a result, I felt inadequate and unworthy.

By the time I went to graduate school, I was ready to latch onto anyone. Thank goodness, the person was my best friend and lifelong lover. Whew. I got lucky there (someone was watching out for me). I could've really gotten myself in trouble. I know so many people who fall in love with anyone who will even act kind for a short period of time and then realize it's not the type of self-giving love they wanted. I've heard some horror stories of "love" turning into demeaning verbal and physical abuse. Just because a person needed to be loved by anyone. But that's why I want to remind you to move beyond neediness.

Love from someone else is extra special when it's a true love. But it doesn't complete you or me or anyone else. To say that it does means that God did not complete the job when creating us. And it belies the evidence that God meets all of our needs. "And my God will supply every need of yours according to his riches in glory in Christ Jesus" (Phil. 4:19). Indeed, God meets all of your needs.

So, if you think you missed out by not having a steady boyfriend, a spouse, or someone special, think again. Perhaps you were called to a different life. In 1 Corinthians 7:7, Paul says, "Sometimes I wish everyone were single like me—a simpler life in many ways! But celibacy is not for everyone any more than marriage is. God gives the gift of the single life to some, the gift of the married life to others." There are gifts that come with marriage and with couples but a different set that comes with being single.

Remember to move beyond neediness. You are all that you need in Christ. Celebrate!

Reflection

1. Are there times when you feel like you need someone else in order to feel complete? What's happening at those times?

2. What gives you a sense of wholeness?

3. What steps can you take to develop self-worth and independence?

BEYOND LONELY

*Our brothers and sisters are there with us from
the dawn of our personal stories to the inevitable dusk.*

Susan Scarf Merrell

Have you had times when you felt so lonely? Even in the midst of a crowd, or at a party, or perhaps even at your place of worship? It feels even worse when you are surrounded by people who do not see what you hold inside. The risk may be too high in those moments to reveal your inner feelings. You wonder, "How can I know so many people and yet be so alone in the world?" "Who can I reach out to who will understand me - even without the right words?"

For me, it is my sister. She is so precious to me. My sister knows me inside and out. She has seen me at my best and at my worst. I have been supportive of her and yet unkind at other times. But my sister forgives because she knows my heart. She has been with me since the beginning.

When I was little and my sister had to babysit me, she would lay me down for a nap. When I awoke, I would find a piece of candy under my pillow. Or she would offer me 25 cents if I would make our bed. I loved that because it meant I could buy candy at the store.

She bragged (and still does) on me telling her friends how smart or gifted or creative I was. And in my darkest hours, I knew who would be there for me. It only took a phone call, and she could tell by the sound of my voice, or if we were together, by the look in my eyes that I was in pain. And she comforted me. She offered me a place where I could freely share knowing that whatever I said or did, she would still love me. Carol Saline says, "Sisters function as safety nets in a chaotic world simply by being there for each other."

Now some of you may not have a biological sister or may not have this type of relationship with your brother or sister. Here's where it can get fun, and yet scary. There is at least one person who can be your sister and provide the type of solace you need that takes you beyond lonely. Think about the people you know.

I also have one of those sisters. She's been my friend and sister for almost 30 years. Like my sister, she also knows my strengths and weakness, my areas of growth, and yet she remains my biggest fan. There have been times when she holds me up. I'm so glad I found a sister of choice.

So now it's your turn. Who helps you get beyond that lonely place? Ecclesiastes 4:9-10 says, "Two are better than one, because they have a good return for their labor: if either of them falls down, one can help the other up. But pity anyone who falls and has no one to help them up." It's time to claim your sister. Go be a sister to someone. Allow someone in to be your sister (or brother). Together the path becomes easier with another beside you than trying to go it alone.

Reflection

1. If you have a brother or sister, in what ways do they give you strength and courage?

2. If you don't have a sibling, who is present in your life who could provide you hope and honesty?

3. What could you do to build that kind of relationship?

_____

_____

_____

_____

_____

BEYOND NOTHINGNESS

*She understood her worth which made her powerful.
The world gravely needed a hero, so she became one.
No superpowers really, just a strong woman
who took no nonsense from anyone.*

Rabdall Core

If you start a journey, you must begin right here with you. What do you know about yourself? I remember a time when I was a young adult, and someone told me to sit down and write who I was besides a mother and wife. I wrote a nice title at the top of the page: WHO AM I? And then I went blank. I didn't know what else to write because I really didn't know. I felt like I'd lost a sense of identity. That left me feeling slightly depressed. Was I really nothing besides a wife and mother? I'd lost my way during my travels to that point.

So, I made more lists. One such list I called WHAT I'VE DONE. That was easier. At that point, I could say that I had a degree in psychology and a degree in theology. I could also say I had worked at a home improvement store, been a housekeeper, and a receptionist. But creating that list stirred something within me and I continued on the path of self-discovery.

My next list was WHAT WOULD PEOPLE SAY ABOUT ME? Now, I had to pause and think about this. This could go bad quickly because my tendency is to focus only on the negative. So I made a simple rule. If I thought of something bad that someone had said about me, then I had to also list something positive. I wanted to maintain my balance. This felt much like walking through a minefield. I had to be careful where I stepped. But I managed this pretty well at the time. People said I was stuck up, reserved, shy, emotional, hard to get along with, and distant. But they also said I was super smart, creative, sensitive and caring. Still, I was uncertain of who I was.

Then I remembered my counselor during seminary gave me a personality inventory because I said I felt out of place in the world. The inventory told me something about myself. My personality occurs in 1% of the American population. Oh, well, that explains something. The counselor told me, "You're an iron fist in a velvet glove." I had to think on that one. But every time I struggled with my self-identity, I came back to this personality profile to understand myself better. I took a lot of other personality tests and learned more about me.

But the most important thing I learned was during my spiritual time. I became increasingly convinced that I was God's creation and that God loved me beyond measure, beyond what others did or thought, and beyond my sense of nothingness. The psalmist says,

> *"Oh yes, you shaped me first inside, then out; you formed me in my mother's womb. I thank you, High God—you're breathtaking! Body and soul, I am marvelously made! I worship in adoration—what a creation! You know me inside and out, you know every bone in my body; You know exactly how I was made, bit by bit, how I was sculpted from nothing into something. Like an open book, you watched me grow from conception to birth; all the stages of my life were spread out before you, The days of my life all prepared before I'd even lived one day"* (Ps. 139:13-16, MSG).

God knows me! And that's when it occurred to me that's really all I need to know. I am deeply and truly known by the Holy One. God knows me in entirety. God created me.

As an amateur artist, I understand what it means to create something from nothing. There's an emotional process that occurs that binds me to that which I have created. And when I declare, "That's really good," it's much harder to part with it when someone wants it. Even more difficult is to see someone treat it without care or to describe it as nothing much. But yet that's what we do to ourselves at times, isn't it?

And so that led me to a sense of conviction. How do I view myself? How do I treat God's wonderful creation? From time to time, I am reminded that I am a miracle, God's miracle. That challenges me to treat myself with respect and honor.

So today, go beyond your claim of nothingness. Treat God's creation with tender, loving care. Declare God's marvelous work - YOU! When you claim your worth, then you are free to move beyond.

Reflection

1. Who are you? Make a list for yourself of your qualities, accomplishments, and values.

2. What do you appreciate most about yourself?

3. What would you like to change?

4. Most important, who is God calling you to be? Write about it on the following page.

BEYOND ME

Life doesn't make any sense without interdependence.
We need each other, and the sooner we learn that, the better for us all.

Erik Erikson

Over the past few weeks I've enjoyed seeing all the photos of children doing school at home or restarting school, especially those of kids entering kindergarten or 1st grade. My grandson started as a kinder this year and I spoke to him that night to see how his first day went. I thought about how this was a new experience, a new school, new teacher, and new friends. It reminded me of my own walk down the sidewalk to 1st grade. My mom offered to walk with me but I was too proud and independent. I refused her but that was a long walk because I was so frightened. Little did I know how predictive that was of my personality - little Miss "I can do it by myself."

That stubborn streak of independence continued as I entered high school and then college. Going into my junior year of college, my mom dropped me off at Texas Woman's University and then went to see my grandma. When she returned a week later, I had transferred across town to the University of North Texas, found a roommate, and rented an apartment. I'm not sure why that surprised her since it was so true to my nature.

Of course, then I moved across the country for graduate school with only $1,000 in my pocket. My parents were so concerned about how I was going to support myself that they had a garage sale to help me with finances. I arrived in San Francisco and within two weeks was set up in the women's dorm, enrolled in classes, and working 10 hours a week as a house cleaner. I made it work.

Moving and attending schools are not all I've done alone. Some are fine accomplishments, like getting two masters and a doctoral degree, doing postgraduate work, writing a musical, making 3 cds on my own, learning to paint. But some have not turned out so well, like the time I decided to paint our house, no, not just one house, but two houses.

The first house I painted on the outside was a small one-story house. My husband came home from work one day to find me with a paintbrush in hand and covered in paint. He wasn't sure what had more paint on it – the house or me. But then I decided to paint our next house which seemed simple at the start. The side I started on was one story. Then I moved to the next side, which was two stories and had a live electrical line feeding into it. Yep, I accidentally touched that, it threw me off the ladder with a blood-curdling scream, and my neighbor at my feet wondering if I needed an ambulance. "No – oo – oo," I said, "I'm okay." I shook for the next few hours. I had to finish the job and so I moved to the back, again two stories, with a rock base. My family came home to see that my ladder had fallen, and the brush marks clearly drew a jagged line from roof to base as I fell with paintbrush in hand. But I wasn't ready for the final side – all three stories. I could never finish that eave and we sold the house with that part unfinished. My husband jokingly said I should get on the roof and lean over to paint it. I said, "I'm not that dumb."

And then my reliance on my ability for home diy projects finally got me in further trouble. I decided I wanted to stain the concrete in my den. I ripped up the carpet, pulled up the nails and plywood, and rented a floor sander. I should have known I was in for trouble when the clerk said, "You need to start in the middle of the room." I heeded his advice but asked for no further help, turning the machine on, and as I moved it slightly, it took me on a ride across the room only to make a 4 inch hole in the wall. As I jerked it away, it headed toward the glass door, so I shifted it again, and it hit another wall knocking a 6 inch hole in the wall. I was screaming for my husband and he walked into the room as I stopped the machine. I thought he was trying to be zen-like when he said, "Did you ever think of letting go?" I didn't realize he meant let go of the machine but, perhaps, the real message was deeper. Sometimes I need to let go of things, or at least go beyond myself to ask for help.

But that need to do it all myself often gets in the way. I can do things more quickly and efficiently by myself plus it's hard to ask for help. The truth is, and I often forget it, sometimes I don't do things well by myself and I really do need help. But my ego or lack of assertiveness interferes with my ability to ask. My husband learned long ago that I'm unlikely to ask for help so on occasion he will ask, "How can I help you?" That is helpful to me. But I'm thinking it's time to grow up now.

Do you have difficulty asking for what you need? I'm reminded that we were created to be in relationship. When God made Adam, God said, "It is not good for man to be alone." And God created Eve. I don't think that was just about husband and wife, but also person to person. We need one another. So why do we try to go it alone so often? Succeeding in life isn't about what I can accomplish on my own but rather about going beyond me to accomplish even more with others. Ryunosuke Satoro said, "Individually, we are one drop. Together, we are an ocean."

Today, think about how you can go beyond yourself. You don't have to do this alone. Ask someone for help.

Reflection

1. How often do you need help with something?

2. In what ways are you able to ask for help?

3. What makes asking for help difficult for you?

4. How can you learn to ask for help? How can you offer help to others?

BEYOND MY NEED

We know that mental illness is not something that happens to other people. It touches us all. Why then is mental illness met with so much misunderstanding and fear?

Tipper Gore

Working in a downtown location is interesting. While I am surrounded by a professional community, I'm also aware of those who are homeless or who have a mental illness. We have a regular tenant on the corner by our building. I don't know much about him but know he's homeless and likely suffers from mental illness. Most people ignore him. At times he's docile and other times he will talk loudly, albeit not to anyone. He usually has a few belongings with him but those change from day to day. Most people ignore him, including me, and go on about their business. One day I saw something that struck me as remarkable. A woman, who was dressed professionally, crossed the street, walked up to this man, called him by name, and inquired about his well-being. As I walked by, I felt such a conflict inside. I've ignored this man for the past two weeks. Should I stop and meet him? Should I also inquire about his needs? And yet that is uncomfortable for me. When people come to me in need, I don't hesitate to find ways to help. But to go outside my comfort zone and reach out to him? I don't know about that. I'm still thinking on that incident, but it did spark something else inside me.

My husband trains ministers to provide pastoral care to people who are in the hospital or hospices or even churches. One of the concepts he explores with these ministers is the degree of self-awareness they possess as well as their motivation for such ministry. If a minister says that he or she prayed for someone, my husband will ask him or her, "Whose need does this meet?" This is to prompt a self-exploration of whether the minister is doing something because the deed makes him or her feel better or satisfied, or whether this act is truly an act of selfless ministry to another person. Many times, it's an act that makes one feel more peaceful that they did something, while other times it's likely meeting the need of both individuals. Less often something is offered that only meets the other person's need. But the point of the exercise is simply to increase one's awareness of self-interest or incentive.

So back to my homeless neighbor. I'm thinking about this act of kindness towards the man and I try to envision myself doing the same. Frankly, I freeze and yet I wonder what's that about? Certainly, I know how to deal with homeless people. I know plenty of places that can be helpful. And obviously, as a mental health professional, I'm not uncomfortable with people with mental illness.

So, where does my discomfort lie? Perhaps it's with the inconvenience. Then I tell myself it's not inconvenient to stop for a few minutes to engage him in conversation, if possible. But then I realize it might be the discomfort of the what ifs. What if one time isn't enough? What if he starts to approach me again, or on multiple occasions? What if he needs more than I can provide? What if it pulls me out of my comfortable place? What if reaching out to him is more about satisfying my need to feel good about helping someone on the street? What if…and the list goes on.

So today I decided to stop and just say hi. But he's gone. He's not at my corner. That concerns me because he's been there every day all day for a long time (so I'm told by my co-workers). I'm worried about him now. I hope someone has shown him a place that is helpful to him. And I'm worried that my ability to do something is now gone (at least, temporarily).

I'm reminded of Proverbs 3:27, "Do not withhold good from those to whom it is due, when it is in your power to act." It was within my power to do something good for this man. My greatest fear in this is being known. What if another homeless person asks me for help, and another, and another? Where will it end? That goes beyond my need. But maybe that's not a bad thing. When it's too much, I am responsible for letting someone know I cannot give more. But today, perhaps I should go beyond my own need for privacy and security and risk giving to someone else.

Reflection

1. Who has God placed in your life that calls you to move beyond your own need and meet the need of another?

2. What is one thing you can do to reach beyond and help someone you might normally avoid?

_____

_____

_____

_____

_____

_____

_____

_____

BEYOND APPEARANCES

Be curious, not judgmental.

Walt Whitman

How do you choose books to read? I'm curious about what people read and how they make those choices, especially in a digital age. Do you look at the bestseller list – which one? Is it word of mouth or something you heard on the radio? How about a book club?

I recently joined one and was already reading the book selected for the month. Since I'm commuting about an hour a day, I decided to listen to audio books again. In the past three weeks, I've completed four books. It's actually been quite fun to listen. And I'm pleasantly surprised. But still, where do I go? How can I judge whether a book is interesting or not? In the past, we would look at the cover, which was actually not a good way to choose a reading and thus the adage, "don't judge a book by its cover."

As I was thinking about this, it reminded me of how often we use appearances to make choices. How do people choose their dating partner? Or their spouse? Or their house, or furniture, office space, restaurant, or friends? Right now, you're probably telling me that you don't use appearance to determine your social group. Really? Let's check this out.

Since the early 70s, social psychologists have collected evidence of our sensitivity to attractive people.[12] We filter to whom we have conversations, activities, and deeper relationships initially by appearance. In other words, we "judge the book by its cover." It's really an automatic process that occurs without much thought. Social psychologists label this the halo effect, meaning that we have tendencies to evaluate others based solely on outer appearance.[13]

Still denying it, aren't you? It's called trait inferences. When we see photos on social media, or when we initially meet people, or perhaps view them across the room, we immediately make a judgment about that person – are they trustworthy? Competent? Intelligent? Likeable? And because we make these choices quickly, we also rule out if, how, and when we might interact with them.[14]

Could we be missing out? Are we overlooking people who could deeply influence us if we moved beyond appearances? How often do you go beyond that first impression to know someone more deeply? There are some people to whom I refer as the beautiful people. We're attracted to them and desire to be in their group.

But is that where we need to be?

In 1 Samuel, God tells Samuel to anoint a king for the Israelites. When questioning how to find someone, here's what happens. "But God told Samuel, 'Looks aren't everything. Don't be impressed with his looks and stature. I've already eliminated him. God judges persons differently than humans do. Men and women look at the face; God looks into the heart'" (1 Sam. 16:7). Those familiar with the story know that Samuel finds David, the youngest and the runt of the family, to become king. Say what? Of course, the story goes on with David slaying the giant Goliath, and becoming best friends with King Saul's son, Jonathan, and then having to run for his life because of Saul's jealousy, becoming King, messing up with Bathsheba, etc. The basic point is that we probably would not have chosen David based on his appearance, or his behaviors later (but that's a different discussion).

God was telling Samuel to move beyond appearances. Could it be that God is telling us the same? Think on this the next few days. In what way are you evaluating others based on appearances? Go beyond.

Reflection

1. As you think about the last few weeks, is there someone that you've ignored because they didn't quite fit your expectations?

2. What is God trying to tell you about others? Write about it on the following page.

BEYOND THE CENTER

*In order to live a fulfilled life,
do not focus on the size of your audience;
focus instead on leaving an impact on the
circle of influence God has given you.*

Rosette Mugidde Wamambe

Earlier today I was discussing this book with my spouse and as I explained where I was going with this, he said, "Oh, I just thought it was a diary of your life and what was happening each week." While that's true, it's far from where I want to go with this, and I explained my idea of going beyond. Recent events in my life gave me time to think about where I've been and where I'm going. In the midst of this, I heard God calling me to a deeper place and a wider sphere of influence. I realized how I isolate myself to a small circle of friends and family. Then I recalled a book on evangelism from years ago called Concentric Circles of Concern. While this blog is not about winning souls, it is about fulfilling God's purposes. Then when speaking with someone about a volunteer activity at church, I remembered what Jesus says in John 17:20 – 23. "My prayer is not for them alone. I pray also for those who will believe in me through their message, that all of them may be one, Father, just as you are in me and I am in you. May they also be in us so that the world may believe that you have sent me. I have given them the glory that you gave me, that they may be one as we are one— I in them and you in me—so that they may be brought to complete unity. Then the world will know that you sent me and have loved them even as you have loved me."

God's desire is that we are in unity – that means that we have a lot of work to do in reconciliation with one another and with God. My challenge is to work that out in a practical matter and so each day I reflect on ways to do that for myself and to call you to do the same. It means going beyond the center of my private world – that place where I'm most comfortable with certain friends and family members.

I suppose I should tell you that I'm introverted by nature so going beyond the center is discomfiting. It stretches me in ways that I don't like and yet know are necessary, both for myself, for you, and the world around us.

Whether introverted or not, all of us socially segregate ourselves. While we form homogeneous groups, we limit ourselves and actually increase segregation, bias, and prejudice. How can we fulfill God's word when we are not fully aware of one another? How can I stand aside and witness others treated unjustly when God calls me to be part of Jesus' ministry. "The Spirit of God, the

Master, is on me because God anointed me. He sent me to preach good news to the poor, heal the heartbroken, announce freedom to all captives, pardon all prisoners" (Isaiah 61). And yet you and I isolate from those witnesses in different arenas.

Oh, you think we don't that? Segregation is still impacting all of us. Did you know that segregation has increased in metropolitan areas over the last 40 years?[15] While we think we're making progress, we're getting further behind. The problem with increasing segregation is that it works subtly, increasing implicit bias, or those attitudes and stereotypes hidden within us that activate involuntarily when making policies, voting, in areas of health care, judicial affairs, and in financial decisions.[16]

Back to the circles. . . the idea that captured my attention was that I could begin with the center and speak to issues of self, then loved ones, and then continue moving outward as I gradually draw myself and you into lives that go beyond comfort and into those areas where things or people seem untouchable. This journey is about pulling us, sort of like pulling taffy, outwardly in a continuous motion, until we are so pliable that going to the fringes to reach all people becomes natural and desirable.

Is this about me alone? Perhaps. Maybe it is a lonely little diary that voyeurs can read. Or, it can be a life-changing vocation that brings us into one accord with God. You choose. Are you going to be a bystander or a life-changer?

Reflection

1. Take a piece of paper and draw concentric circles (circles within circles). Think about the influences you have beginning with those people closest to you. Continue to fill these circles in as you make your way to the outer circles.

2. Who do you need to add? Are there people or groups of people that you need to reach?

3. What is God saying to you about being a difference maker?

_____

_____

_____

_____

_____

_____

_____

BEYOND HURT

In order to be free, we must learn how to let go.
Release the hurt. Release the fear.
Refuse to entertain the old pain.

Mary Manin Morrissey

Have you ever had pain? For those who have, you know how it can absorb your whole being. The ever-present discomfort constantly steals your thoughts and emotions. It's difficult to focus and even harder to conceive of life beyond the suffering. I admire people who continue to live abundantly despite their present pain. I don't do as well.

There are many different types of distress – physical and emotional. Some we bring upon ourselves and others fall upon us. Suffering is not new to humans. The evidence of hurt is a theme throughout the Bible. Whether it's pain from betrayal (Psalm 41:9, "Even my close friend in whom I trusted, who ate my bread, has lifted his heel against me"), or loss (Luke 11:35, "Jesus wept"), or great suffering (Job 30:20, "I cry out to you, God, but you do not answer").

When we suffer, our tendency is to pull away and isolate. I remember hearing people say they left church because of something that happened that was painful. Or have observed how families will split, and not even remember why it occurred. Sometimes the breach feels too great and so people walk away. But this becomes isolating. How many times can you walk away? And does it make the hurt disappear?

I was thinking about this when talking with someone recently. She and a family member have not spoken in 15 years. But this person decided to call up this family member and they had a wonderful conversation. This made my heart both glad and yet so sad as I have been unable to reach reconciliation in all of my own damaged relationships. It's a goal all of us must move towards.

But what of the suffering caused by a group, an organization, a culture, or the world at large? How can we ever move towards reconciliation? This led me to write a song. Part of it says,

> *Together we can reach the fringes, all those who feel apart. Perhaps it won't be easy, but it will prove God's tender heart. So pull together, embrace each other, accept another way. As one in voice, in spirit, in love, a movement for the day.*
> Going beyond hurt means that I take the first step.

Jesus' words echo, "Take up your bed and walk." As I look around and see myself sitting in my ashes of agony, and heaping them upon myself, I realize that God calls me to rise up, and move towards others. It's so very difficult to move forward when you're walking in pain but the alternative is worse.

Henri Nouwen refers to us as wounded healers. He reminds us that suffering is universal and it is in that shared experience that we enter into communion with one another. Our differences are no longer things that are aberrant but rather creative. Nouwen says it best, "All this suggests that when one has the courage to enter where life is experienced as most unique and most private, one touches the soul of the community."[17]

I've packed up my bed, have you? Today, move beyond the hurt. Become a wounded healer.

Reflection

1. In what ways have you been wounded in the past?

2. What have you done to move beyond the hurt?

3. Who have you hurt?

4. What have you done to repair your relationships?

BEYOND REGRET

Be the hero of hearts; learn to say I'm sorry.

Richelle E. Goodrich

Have you ever broken something precious or valuable? Or perhaps something which held fondness? Recently a sermon on regret made me stop and think. In what way do regrets become a barrier to moving beyond? As I've reflected on that this week, I've realized that they become a stumbling block. I had an opportunity to test it this week at a conference.

My friends saved me a seat at lunch since I was busy answering questions after my conference talk. When I walked into the banquet room, the seat saved was at their table but on the opposite side of them. That wasn't a problem for me until I saw the seat was next to someone with whom my last encounter about 15 years ago was deeply wounding and left me with some scars. My anxiety began to rise, and I started to walk away looking for a different spot to sit. Then I heard that still, small voice within me say, "Go and be compassionate." After all, I'd just spoken about the need for us to be kind and understanding of one another. and to practice self-compassion. So, I did. I sat beside this woman and greeted her warmly and cordially. I inquired about her work and her life. We had a good, friendly conversation. More than that, a sense of peace flooded me as I sat beside her and silently said, "May she be kind. May she be kind to herself. May she have compassion. May she have peace."

The relationship with her and that place of work has been a source of regret for me. I am saddened by the way I handled the situation, the people, and myself. But after last week's sermon, in which the pastor referred to 1 John 1:9, "If we confess our sins, he is faithful and just and will forgive us our sins and purify us from all unrighteousness," I realized at a heart level that the only person who hasn't forgiven me is probably me. I need to do that, practice some self-compassion, and move on.

I have lots of regrets. I've made a lot of mistakes. But in my practice of self-crucifixion, I argue with God about my personhood, God's ability to forgive, and my refusal to accept that forgiveness, and then continue to live full of shame and fear that I'll mess up again. That, my friends, keeps me from living the abundant life which I'm promised.

During that sermon, I cried. I wept for how unforgiving I am of myself. The tears flowed gently down my face as I watched people going to the alter seeking resolution of their own regrets. And my heart was touched as I watched the ministers, especially a female minister, reach out and bring this message from God to those of us who struggle with forgiveness. My husband gently put his arm around me and in that communicated his forgiveness of my humanness.

So, this week I've tried to walk in this forgiveness, and in so doing, am finding forgiveness and love for others. My challenge is to continue moving beyond regret. How about you? Isn't it time for you to do the same?

Reflection

1. What things have you done that you regret?

2. What people have you injured along the way?

3. In what ways have you forgiven yourself? others?

4. How have you apologized to those you hurt?

_____

_____

_____

_____

_____

BEYOND SADNESS

What brings us to tears, will lead us to grace.
Our pain is never wasted.

Bob Goff

One of my favorite courses to teach for a nursing school is bioethics in which we discuss topics like worldview, moral status theories, the Christian narrative and how that informs medical care, along with examining case studies of fetal abnormality, conflicting ethical principles, and terminal illness. Both classes recently discussed death and dying. Students shared their experiences at hospitals and the frequency with which they must face the death of a pane of my favorite courses to teach for a nursing school is bioethics in which we discuss topics like worldview, moral status theories, the Christian narrative and how that informs medical care, along with examining case studies of fetal abnormality, conflicting ethical principles, and terminal illness. Both classes recently discussed death and dying. Students shared their experiences at hospitals and the frequency with which they must face the death of a patient. But my favorite part is to hear the personal stories of students who have lost a loved one and how they work through that. No matter the story, the common theme is sadness. I treat these with special care knowing that grief is an individual journey.

In these classes I share my perspective about how grief can't be defined by stages and that, in fact, any theory which tries to promote stages of grief has been debunked. There's no empirical evidence that people go through stages of grief. Dr. George Bonanno, a bereavement researcher, says, "People go through this sort of oscillation period where they go in and out of states of deep sadness, and that gradually lessens, and they move on."[18] During the 80s, Dr. Bonanno noticed that people don't follow a grief pattern and notes that the concept of grief stages was developed upon observation of those who were dying but not people who were grieving the loss of a loved one. It was then popularized by media and applied to all forms of grief. The problem with viewing grief as stage-like is when someone doesn't follow what is considered "normal" grieving and then is pathologized. Working in several hospices, I can recall how often staff would say, "She's in denial."

No matter how hard I try to re-educate folks, they really have a hard time letting go of this idea. My concern is not so much with an order to things but with the idea that we can tell people how they "ought" to grieve. I remember doing a radio show in the early 90s where I spoke of grief and how stages are an inaccurate way to describe what happens. Talking about stages really creates confusion, isn't proven, and is potentially damaging to those who are bereaved.[19] Then Stroebe and Schut proposed a different theory, much like what Dr. Bonanno describes, that of moving back and forth between different types of coping, one focused on loss and the other on restoration.[20] This not only made more sense to me but also described my own experiences with loss.

Throughout the years, my husband and I have had many opportunities to view and aid people in this process since he is a chaplain and I am a therapist and served as a hospice chaplain. My own experiences have been plentiful since my father died when I was 7, my grandparents died when I was young, my son died, my brother died, followed by my mother-in-law, my father, and just this week, my father-in-law. Each time was different.

I'm sitting in sadness and yet happiness knowing that my father-in-law, who was 94, a decorated veteran, a committed Christian and Sunday school teacher, lived a full life. And yet I do feel the loss, not only because he is gone but because it represents so many other things which I have lost. It's as if grief is cumulative, creating deeper pockets of sadness within me.

I'm also sad thinking about my stepdad, Buddy, who died a few years back and about others I love who are currently fighting for their life.

And yet, I am called to live a life that celebrates those who are alive. In Matthew 8:22, Jesus says, "Let the dead bury the dead." Was he telling us not to grieve? Of course not. When Lazarus died, Jesus wept (John 11:35). However, Jesus was trying to help a man respond to his immediate calling, one which had eternal value, and help the follower understand that he was rationalizing his neglect or refusal to respond to Jesus' invitation. At times I've seen people who remained so focused on their loss, that they couldn't or wouldn't move on to fulfill their purpose in life. In my mind, our sorrow and realization of the importance of relationships can serve to deepen our calling and enrich the meaning for that we serve.

So, today and probably for a while, I will wear my funeral attire, and I will process these uncomfortable feelings that come with loving and losing. But I know also that I will integrate this and weave it into the fabric of my life as I continue to live out God's calling in me. I invite you to sit with me for a few moments and then move beyond sadness.

Reflection

1. What grief are you facing today? Have you lost someone you loved?

2. In what ways is grief touching your life because of the crisis?

3. What has helped you in your previous times of grief? What do you need now?

BEYOND SUCCESS

The pessimist sees difficulty in every opportunity.
The optimist sees opportunity in every difficulty.

Winston Churchill

How is this situation changing your view of success? Is it causing you to re-think your priorities? What does it mean to be successful? Someone told me recently, "I'm realizing that my view of success is totally different than my supervisor's view. I have many more expectations of myself than she does." I spoke of students who cry in dismay at receiving a 99 on an exam instead of 100. My response is usually, "Your grade in this class will be a letter, not a number." I can't even count the number of clients whose idea of achievement is perfection and so lead less than happy lives because of this. I must admit that I fall prey to this as well. Sometimes I focus only on the mistakes I make, and I tend to view these as failures and that messes with my head. I need to heed my own advice and focus on what I do accomplish.

Several of these conversations this week led me to read more about this. Why are we so unhappy and unable to focus on our successes? In his book, *If You're So Smart, Why Aren't You Happy?*, Raj Raghunathan speaks to this. He says we only need three things to be happy: "great social relationships, a sense of purpose, and a 'positive' attitude toward life."[21] However, Dr. Raghunathan tells us the question is a bit more complicated than that. Simply knowing those three things don't automatically create satisfaction. We're curious human beings and we need to understand why those things matter and we need to understand the situations or things that trigger our unhappiness. As he discusses in his book, he outlines the following killers of happiness: devaluing happiness, chasing superiority, desperation for love, being overly controlling, distrusting others, the indifferent pursuit of passion, and mind addiction.[22]

While I haven't read the entire book, some of this makes sense to me. How often have I negated significantly happy moments and instead focused on the times when I feel less than happy? Or how about those times when it's not enough to achieve something but rather I want to outdo someone else? I could go on with my own faulty cognitions and actions, but I think that many of us do these things.

What makes us happy? Where do we find the abundant life that Jesus mentions in John 10:10? Now, you want to give a sweet church answer like "You just need to rely on God," or "Pray more, read your Bible, more quiet time."

And I'm not arguing against those things. What I'm really after is digging deeper to move beyond our human idea of success. Some propose that we need to laugh more (that sounds fun).[23] Others tell us just to think more positively. Other studies indicate that mindfulness-based practices will make us feel better.[24] I'm not doubting that any of these are true.

I wonder if we simply need to re-define success. If that happens, then that will change our degree of happiness. I started thinking about how God defines success. Micah 6:8 (MSG) says, "But he's already made it plain how to live, what to do, what God is looking for in men and women. It's quite simple: Do what is fair and just to your neighbor, be compassionate and loyal in your love, and don't take yourself too seriously— take God seriously." Huh. Let's think about this.

What would it look like for us to practice justice? I'm thinking of someone I know who is an attorney and is passionate about issues of justice. I watch her in wonder as she finds ways to engage in creating justice and encouraging the rest of us to find opportunities to bring justice. What would it mean for us to practice fairness in our lives, in our work, in our neighborhood? Perhaps it's just one small thing like picking up my neighbor's paper when it's raining and placing it on their doorstep. Or opening a door for someone. Or volunteering to take a co-worker's on-call weekend.

What does it look like to practice compassion and kindness towards ourselves and others? It's a reminder to take a deep breath and offer a gentle hand or a caring smile. How about returning that phone call, email, or text message? What about buying someone a cup of coffee? Maybe it's paying for another person's order in the drive-up lane. Or how about using that precious commodity called time? Spend time with someone. And how can we practice humility? Maybe it's not so important that I get ahead of someone else but rather I step behind them. And I really like Eugene Patterson's paraphrase: maybe we need to take ourselves less seriously.

So, this week, look around you for ways to bring justice, to be compassionate, to take yourself less seriously, and to focus a little more on God. Go beyond success.

Reflection

1. In what ways do you need to re-define success? Does it mean working more or less?

2. In what ways do you think more about personal success than you do about relationship success?

BEYOND ANXIETY

Anxiety's like a rocking chair.
It gives you something to do, but it doesn't get you very far.

Jodi Picoult

Our church previously announced an upcoming series on anxiety. The minute I heard this I became anxious. Whenever the church attempts to address mental health issues, my first reaction is concern about how that will happen. Religion has not been kind to people with mental health issues. During the 19th century, religious organizations had the primary responsibility for caring for those with mental health illness and treatments were often unkind. One can hear stories of people whom the church has reprimanded, rejected, or isolated because of their mental health issues. There are times when churches or church leaders contribute to an increase in an individual's mental health issues, for example, when sin is linked to anxiety or depression.

Other times, people have experienced the church minimizing their symptoms, telling the people simply to change how they think about things or that they "just need to trust God more." Other times intense religious experiences have resulted in psychotic breaks with those who had an underlying mental health condition such as bipolar disorder or schizophrenia.[25]

Having said all this, religion can be good for mental health when it provides a sense of purpose and meaning, and when people are offered the support they need. Religious practices like praying and meditation can be particularly helpful, as examined by Newburg.[26] There are further studies that indicate that religious coping helps mediate the problems related to mental health by providing a sense of connection through community and encouraging beliefs that focus on trust, the faithfulness of God, and one's purpose in life.[27] At Duke University Medical Center, Dr. Harold G. Koenig and his team discovered that people who are religious have fewer symptoms of depression.[28]

There is a paucity of research on religion and anxiety. Studies thus far have revealed mixed results indicating that religion may or may not be helpful or hurtful. While religious coping may help with trauma or PTSD, it may not be so with generalized anxiety disorder or obsessive-compulsive disorder (OCD).[29] Koenig and his colleagues found in half of their studies that people who were religious had lower levels of anxiety; however, still studies some produced mixed results and some indicated increased symptoms of anxiety related to religion.[30] There are problems with these studies, one of which is that none of these studies are specifically designed to differentiate religious belief systems or practices. The question for those of us who are Christian becomes does my relationship with God or the cognitive belief system or spiritual practices of Christianity have the possibility of decreasing my symptoms of anxiety?

To that question, I respond, "It depends." If a Christian religious group minimizes anxiety by categorizing it as sinful, or thinking of all anxiety as the same, then it can be hurtful. That is a lack of recognition in the church that while we may use the same word to describe what a person experiences, the etiology of different forms of anxiety matter. What is causing the anxiety? To be helpful, we need to consider that is a more complicated issue than simply how one thinks or one's self talk. To be certain, core beliefs are a part of the problem. After all, I am a cognitive-behavioral therapist. My interventions consist of schema exploration and re-development. But, that's only a part of what drives anxiety. Other factors include genetic components or predisposition, adverse childhood experiences which alter the neurocircuitry of the brain, problems related to neurotransmitters, traumatic experiences, medication, life stressors, and drug or alcohol use.

My need to speak about this, as a mental health professional, comes from the many patients who have come to me over the past 30 years who have tried what their church or pastor suggested and still find themselves with an anxiety disorder that is wreaking havoc on their life, their work, and their family. And now, added to that, they have a sense of guilt and condemnation because they didn't do it the "right" way according to their perception of what their church or minister stated. This only intensifies their symptoms.

My desire is that churches promote a well-balanced view of mental health symptoms and recognize that there are many pathways to treating or curing those conditions. Undoubtedly, people with mental health concerns such as anxiety need a spiritual foundation and religious support group. They may also need medication or other medical protocol to correct issues of neurocircuitry, or a Christian therapist to provide research-based interventions. In fact, my hope is that all of these are employed by people and encouraged by our churches.

In the meantime, I'm still seeking ways to manage my anxiety, or fear, about how our churches practice justice and compassion with anxious people. I move forward and support that my church recognizes the problem and is attempting to talk openly about it. I pray for my ministers that they will have wisdom and discernment. And I pray that the people will be able to move beyond anxiety.

Reflection

1. Think about your own anxiety. Do you commonly experience anxiety on a daily or weekly basis?

2. What fuels that anxiety? How does it cause barriers in your relationships?

3. What helps you most when you are anxious?

_____

_____

_____

_____

_____

_____

_____

BEYOND THE BLACK BOX

The art of acceptance is the art of making someone who has done you a small favor wish that he might have done you a greater one.

Martin Luther King, Jr.

The FDA requires that any prescription drug have a label that alerts the user to any serious or life-threatening risks. It's called commonly called a "black box warning." There are times when people express concern because they tell the user all the potential side effects. It can be quite frightening to read, but the aim is to let the patient know that any of those might happen or may not happen at all. It's basically a "heads up" and reminds all of us to remain alert to new symptoms or reactions.

So due to some recent situations I've encountered, I was thinking that people should carry black box warnings so we could be aware of the potential dangers or dilemmas when we interact with them. These might be some that we think during this time:

> "Be careful. Her niece has a cold." "Watch out, he works with the homeless people." "Stay away. I saw her cough."

Or how about these?

> "Beware. This person can be moody." "Watch out. Snaps your head off if you interfere with her task." "Slow down. He's about to sell you a swamp in Florida."

Or maybe these.

> "Be quiet. He or she will talk about you behind your back." "Don't be forthright. This person will tell someone else that you may or may not want to know this information." "Be careful. This person is passive-aggressive. They will agree with you and then complain about you later."

I think you get the picture. I'm just thinking it would be helpful to have a "heads up" about people, particularly those you don't really know well. I even started to design a badge people could wear on their lapel (just kidding).

But then I got worried because I'm afraid of what my warning label might have on it. As I told my new boss recently, there's a lot of people in this town who think I'm the best thing since sliced bread but then there are people who can't stand me and would rather not have anything to do with me.

I hope that's not true for any of you. I know that I have the type of personality that can be aggravating at times. My husband is always telling me to stay under the radar, yet he knows he's asking the impossible. I'm honest with my thoughts and feelings. That could be bad or good. I couldn't even lie if I wanted to because my face won't allow it. My expressions tell the whole story. And I tried keeping my thoughts to myself at one point in time and I became physically ill trying to do that. So, I decided you either love me or hate me. At least I know where I stand, most of the time.

Except with new acquaintances. Thus, the need for a black box warning on both of us. We need to know what we're getting into, don't we?

However, I have learned some things in life. People have different perspectives of the same person. We don't think alike, do we? You may love some people that I have no desire to be around and vice versa. So that warning thing might not work. Plus, it would cause us to pre-judge a person. Somedays we like a person and the next day we don't like them, depending on the circumstance, or their mood, or our disposition. I'm reminded of how we are all created in God's image. "God spoke: 'Let us make human beings in our image, make them reflecting our nature' . . .God looked over everything he had made; it was so good, so very good" (Gen. 1:26–27, 31. MSG). That's all of us, folks! Every single one of us is made after God's likeness, bearing God's characteristics. We are all very good! But do we see one another that way?

I'll tell you this is stretching me because there are a few folks that I'm irritated with and I don't want to see them as God sees them. They bother me. I don't agree with what they say or what they do. I really don't want anything to do with them. However, the Holy Spirit is ever present in my life, speaking to me, and saying, "See them as God sees them." I want to argue, "No!" I don't do that because the conviction of the Spirit reminds me that the fault I see in them is no different than my own. Jesus says, "Don't pick on people, jump on their failures, criticize their faults— unless, of course, you want the same treatment. That critical spirit has a way of boomeranging. It's easy to see a smudge on your neighbor's face and be oblivious to the ugly sneer on your own. Do you have the nerve to say, 'Let me wash your face for you,' when your own face is distorted by contempt? It's this whole traveling road-show mentality all over again, playing a holier-than-thou part instead of just living your part. Wipe that ugly sneer off your own face, and you might be fit to offer a washcloth to your neighbor" (Mt. 7:3-5, MSG). (And she makes the motion of stabbing her heart). Yes, Lord. I love you and I will work on me before I try to work on my brother.

Who are you trying to judge this week? Try to see them as God sees them – Imago Dei. My prayer for all is that we move beyond the black box.

Reflection

1. How does God desire you view others?

2. How can you be accepting and yet protect yourself at the same time?

3. How can you demonstrate God's love and acceptance to others during this time?

_____

_____

_____

_____

_____

BEYOND RUMORS

Words have no wings but they can fly a thousand miles.

Korean Proverb

It's easy to fool ourselves that gossip isn't flying around when we're socially distancing. Think about it. We're still communicating, just in a different way.

I remember a great illustration about gossip from the movie, Doubt, in which Philip Seymour Hoffman, playing a priest, preaches a powerful sermon. He tells of a woman who confesses her gossip habit. The woman asks for forgiveness but before the priest will offer forgiveness, he tells her this, "Not so fast. I want you to go home, take a pillow upon your roof, cut it open with a knife, and return to me." The woman does so and upon her return to confession seeks forgiveness. The priest then asks what happened and she tells him the feathers flew everywhere. Then he says to her, "Now I want you to go back and gather up every last feather that flew out into the wind." When she proclaims that is impossible, the priest says, "And that is gossip!"

We are prone to make assumptions based upon rumors that we hear. This is especially true when the gossip feels like it threatens us. Here's how I describe this to clients.

The total picture of your life includes four areas:

1. Your stuff – those things that you believe belong to you. It could be your possessions, home, car, or your physical body.

2. Your places – where you work, where you go to church, where you like to eat, where you work out, any organization or institution that's important to you.

3. Your people – friends, family, colleagues, people who are vital in your life.

4. Your ideas and values – your philosophy of life, your theology, your decisions, your spiritual side.

All of these compose who you are as a person. If someone says or does something that even hints of disloyalty, disapproval, rejection, abandonment, betrayal, or anything potentially negative or damaging to your stuff, your places, your people, or your ideas/values, then you will do what you think is necessary to protect yourself. You do this because you feel threatened. That fear may come out looking like anger, or you may hide, or you may fight or run. (Sounds like that autonomic system is working well, right?)

Sometimes when I feel threatened, I try to deflect that by talking about others. It's so wrong, I know. I make myself feel less anxious by gossiping about someone else. Plus, it helps to validate my feelings and serves the purpose of "surrounding the camp." And, guess what? They do that about me, or my family, or my people, as well. Every single person spreads a rumor at least once. I thought I'd dig a little deeper on this. Here's some interesting facts from research.

1. There is little empirical evidence that women gossip more frequently than men.[31]

2. One purpose of gossip is to establish or maintain friendships.[32]

3. Extraverts gossip the most and tend to score higher on agreeableness.[33]

4. The average person gossips about 52 minutes a day.[34]

In addition, I found the following four motives for gossip:

1. To influence others and potentially manipulate information in a negative direction.

2. To gather information and validate the information.

3. It's fun. It serves a social need for connection.

4. It protects and group and its norms against harmful behaviors from others outside the group.[35]

There's a lot of interesting information there. However, the main point that I want to get back to is that we desire to believe what we think is true about a person or a group and so end up looking for information from others that confirms those thoughts while ignoring or deflecting information that disconfirms our opinion.

That sounds biased, doesn't it? I wonder what would happen if we treated people like scientists treat research. In empirical sciences, we start with a hunch or suspicion. Let's say our hunch is "Mary steals from the candy basket at work." Maybe someone saw Mary take a chocolate bar but didn't put money in the basket. So, she stole, right? Hmm. Let's see.

If we're scientists, we develop a null hypothesis. That can't be the same as our hunch. To be objective and fair, our null hypothesis would state that Mary does not steal candy. And then we set up a series of experiments to prove or disprove our theory. We may use observation – someone spies on Mary. We might use a counter to keep track of candy bars and times when Mary is in the office. There's a lot of ways we do that, but we will only know if our suspicion is true if we cannot prove our null hypothesis. In other words, if we can't prove that Mary never steals, then we can suggest that perhaps she does. But that leads us down another experiment trail.

If we treated people and groups like experiments, then when we heard a rumor or gossip about them, we would try to disprove that notion. If someone tells me something bad about you, then I should look for contrary evidence. Or, better yet, how about the biblical route?

If someone tells me something bad about you, what if I said, "Hey, I'm so sad that you were treated unfairly by that person. Have you talked to them about it? That might be a good idea." And, then you would go to that person directly, confront them lovingly, and listen to their response. WOW! What a concept. It's the psychologically healthy thing to do.

Jesus tells us, "If a fellow believer hurts you, go and tell him – work it out between the two of you. If he listens, you've made a friend. If he won't listen, take one or two others along so that the presence of witnesses will keep things honest, and try again. If he still won't listen, tell the church. If he won't listen to the church, you'll have to start over from scratch, confront him with the need for repentance, and offer again God's forgiving love" (Mt. 18:15-17). Whoa, back up a minute. You mean if someone offends me, I should go talk to them? Yep. And, that means I shouldn't go gossip about them? Yep. Huh, go figure.

I'm getting long-winded here, but I do want to say that I'm as guilty as you in this. Friends, can we please try to be both healthy and biblical in our relationships? Let's move beyond rumors.

Reflection

1. During this time when you cannot see your friends face-to-face, what are you saying to them in other forms of communication?

2. In what ways do you gossip about others?

3. What harm have you done to others by speaking or writing ill of them?

4. How can you change this and make it right?

BEYOND STUCK

*You may not control all the events that happen to you,
but you can decide not to be reduced by them.*

Maya Angelou

It's done. Or should I say two are done? I made this sweeping declaration in September that I was writing three books and they would be ready by December 1st. And then I thought, "Oh, dear, what have I done to myself?" So I wrote two books in two months. They won't be best sellers. That's not the goal anyway. The aim was to write a book from start to finish. The first book, *Discovery Teaching Like Jesus*, was a joint venture between my spouse and myself. Just in case you're wondering. We've been talking about concepts of teaching adults in church for about 20 years. So coming up with information wasn't as difficult as I expected. But about 40 - 50 pages in, I announced to my husband, "I'm out of words. I don't think there's anything else to say. We don't really have a book." I was stuck. He said, "That's ok. You don't have to write a book." But, oh my, I made a public announcement about it. I HAD to write at least one book. Then, lo and behold, I did more research and discovered an article based on our book. LOL. Ok, actually our ideas were already summarized in the article. So, I wrote some more, and I kept writing every single day. I found more research, information, and resources. I contacted the author of the first article, and he offered to review our manuscript. And I kept writing. By the end of 6 weeks, we had a book. It's not long but it's a real book. The first copy I held in my hands felt so good. To top it off, there are people who are interested in the book. How much better can it get?

Then I thought, "Uh oh, I promised two more books." So, I started the other book. The second was with my sister. Actually, that book was started in July and then a shoulder injury prevented me from completing it earlier. But my sister and I finished that book, *Essential Drops for Living*. Again, I made myself write every single day. When I became stuck, I would read more, do more research, and let the book simmer, just like a pot of stew. I couldn't get the 3rd book done by the first of December, but I finished it two months later, just in time for Valentine's Day. It's called *Essential Drops for Love*. I'm hoping it will help marriages.

So happy ending, right? Not quite yet. Because now I'm stuck in another way. While I let myself experience a wee bit of satisfaction, I started reading the first book. I found typing errors, formatting errors, and then one night after reading most of the book, I thought, "This thing is a mess. I'm not sure I know what I'm saying. It's confusing." Then I felt embarrassed that I so proudly passed out copies. I was stuck in the middle of my perfectionism. I told my husband, "I can't read this book anymore. It's not what I want it to be." He said, and characteristically so, "That's ok. You wrote a book - that was your goal." Ah, I wish I could be that content with something. I corrected the errors and resubmitted it so the next copies will be correct. And then I found more mistakes. Ugh. Will it never end? And in my head, I keep re-arranging information so our information will be clearer. Maybe a 2nd version, an expanded version will come. It feels awful to be stuck.

I laid it aside a few days. Today I picked it up and read some again. And, you know what? I liked it. I still found mistakes, and I know there's room for improvement, but I really love this book and am highlighting those statements that are most profound for me. Maybe, just maybe, I'm moving beyond stuck.

How about you? Are you feeling stuck right now? Isaiah 18b - 19 (GNTB) says, "Do not cling to events of the past or dwell on what happened long ago. Watch for the new thing I am going to do. It is happening already - you can see it now! I will make a road through the wilderness and give you streams of water there." WOWZERS! Isn't that exciting?! God is already working ahead of you, and me, and our "stuckness." He is making the road clear, and at the end will provide the refreshment we need. I can already taste the cool spring water waiting for me ahead, can you?

My friends, be encouraged. You are not at the end of the journey yet. God is paving the way for you. So, today, let's make a commitment together. Let's support one another and move beyond stuck.

Reflection

1. During this time, how are you feeling stuck or trapped?

2. What message is God trying to tell you to help you move beyond this?

3. What changes does God want to do in you?

_____

_____

_____

_____

BEYOND BAD NEWS

Tough times never last, but tough people do.

Robert H. Schuller

It was awful. "There something I need to tell you." My heart starts pounding, my throat tightens, the room starts to spin, and I find myself staring through him into the layers of another world. I'm suspended in air, like the trapeze artist, the flyer, whose lost her grip on the bar and is spiraling through the air, but in slow motion. Slow enough to understand that there is nothing beneath me to break the eventual plummet to the ground. Confusion, fear, and doubt pulse in my swollen head as I search for something, one thing, that I can grab to prevent the precipitous plunge.

That phrase alone is a harbinger for me. One might say that's the wrong word. Originally the word meant providing lodging, perhaps for someone on a journey. However, Shakespeare used the same word to speak of two different senses, the one looking for lodging and the one announcing an arrival.[36] I suppose both fit in my free flung twirling because I'm looking for a safe place while he is pronouncing what is yet to come.

Before you deem me mentally incompetent, let me explain why those words assail me. But, first, how do you respond when someone delivers bad news to you? "Your mother died." "You have stage IV cancer, inoperable." "The company is closing. Today is your last day." Whatever the neon sign, does it feel like someone just punched you in the gut?

Those words, "there's something I need to tell you," "there's something else," "I need to tell you," all precipitate the enunciation of something horrid, bad, nothing that I want, but all that is flying in my face. "Your baby is dying." Crash." "Dad died this morning." Boom." "Today's your last day." Bang. Please, if you have something to tell me, just blurt it right out. Don't set me up for a physiological roller coaster.

We've all had our share of bad news. And it's not the moment in time we fondly recall, and yet it's the memory that refuses to fade. You're thinking about your own times, aren't you? Think about this one. A young man, full of promise, engaged to marry a lovely lady, finds out that she's pregnant (Matthew 1:18-19). Oh, and it's not his baby, uh, and it's in a culture that stones women for such. Oops. Like all innocent men, trying to save his own neck, and yet a nice guy, he contrives a plan to secretly divorce her upon their marriage. Hopefully, that will save her from disgrace. So, the answer is do the right thing – marry her – and then divorce her? Oh, and in a culture that disdains divorced women. Hmm. Things aren't looking so good. Of course, that's not the end of the story. But before we get there, it's important that we see Joseph, like me, hovering in mid-air, desperately looking for a soft place to land. It's not unfamiliar to us, is it? That awful, painful split of a second where our flight or fight system charges in to protect us. Do you put up your fists? Do you run? Do you freeze?

There's a Taoist tale of a farmer whose horse runs away. While his neighbor offers sympathy, "such bad luck," the farmer replies, "Could be bad. Could be good." The horse returns with a dozen wild mares. "Ah, such good luck," remarks the neighbor. "Could be good. Could be bad," responds the farmer. The next day, the farmer's son is thrown off one of the wild horses and breaks his leg. "Tsk, tsk. Such bad luck," offers the neighbor. Unphased, the farmer says, "Could be bad. Could be good." Later that day, the battle call for all able-bodied young men to report for war duty goes out but the farmer's son is ineligible because of his injured leg.[37] So how do we know what's bad news?

In the 1978 novel and 1998 movie, What Dreams May Come, Annie plays chess with her husband, Chris. As she keeps losing, she tells him she wants to keep playing until she wins. She's not one for losing. Unfortunately, the loss is greater for Annie when both of her children are killed in an automobile wreck. Annie tries to commit suicide but is saved. At the hospital, Annie remarks that she lost, meaning she didn't succeed at suicide. Chris tells her, "Sometimes when you lose, you win." Like the Taoist story, winning is defined in different ways.

Back to our companion, Joseph, and his dilemma. An angel appears to him in a dream. "Joseph, son of David, don't hesitate to get married. Mary's pregnancy is Spirit-conceived. God's Holy Spirit has made her pregnant. She will bring a son to birth, and when she does, you, Joseph, will name him Jesus – 'God saves' – because he will save his people from their sins" (Matthew 1:23-23). Whew, I bet that made him feel better. I can picture him at the local hangout the next day with his friends. "Yeah, my fiancé is preggo but, hey, it's all okay. Some guy, like an angel or something, appeared in my dream last night and told me this baby's something else. Gonna be important." Ok, now. That's going to fly, right? So, Joseph's problem isn't really solved. But and let me tell you, it's a big, flying through the air kind of BUT, that's not the end of the story. You and I know the end of that story and it all works out pretty good. However, there's an awful lot of faith-walking that has to take place, which Joseph does. He follows God's instructions despite the moral, legal, and socio-political consequences.

There are times in hearing bad things that we want to be like the little boy in *Alexander and the Terrible, Horrible, No Good, Very Bad*

Day.[38] We want to pack up and move to Australia! It's hard to remember that the proclamation, or situation, or difficult thing is not the end of the story.

Before my baby was born, God came to me in a dream warning me to "hang on and not let go." When my baby was born with meningitis, I was told he would be just fine in a few weeks. A day later, the doctor said, "Call your husband. There's something I need to tell you." When my husband arrived, the doctor gave us the poor prognosis. A few months later, the hospital connected me with another young woman whose baby was stillborn. As we shared the universal pain, she said, "Isn't this the worst thing that's ever happened to you?" I hesitated and then softly replied, "Yes, (pause), and no. It's horrible, tragic, life changing. But it's also magnificent, wonderful, because my baby is in heaven with our Heavenly Father. And he promises that I will be with him again." Then I shared the Grand Narrative of Scripture with this woman. I wanted her to see that sometimes when you lose, you win.

You're dealing with bad news all around. There's something important to remember. You know, the trapeze artist isn't alone up there. Every flyer has a catcher. The flyer's job is to fling him or herself out and away from the swing into mid-air, arms thrust out, trusting that the catcher will be there for him or her. As he relays this story, Nouwen says, "Don't be afraid. Remember that you are the beloved child of God. He will be there when you make your long jump. Don't try to grab him; he will grab you. Just stretch out your arms and hands and trust, trust, trust."[39] Today, my friends, fly, fly, fly into the bad news, the omen, the announcement, and trust, trust, trust. Move beyond the bad news.

Reflection

1. How has God used the most difficult times in your life to bring about something good?

2. In what ways has God been faithful to you?

3. How can you rely upon God's hope and promises today?

_____

_____

_____

_____

_____

BEYOND HARMFUL WORDS

Words are seeds that do more than blow around.
They land in our hearts and not the ground.
Be careful what you plant and careful what you say.
You might have to eat what you planted one day.

Unknown

Falling, tumbling, running over and out, spilling everywhere, and dripping off the table. Pick a flimsy receptacle, one of thin cardboard, like we used to do at camp for water, and place your mug of mocha in it, and pretty soon someone will wonder where that dark stain on your shirt came from. Holding too loosely to a mug can also be dangerous, especially when a toy magically appears out of nowhere, too small to notice, but big enough to trip a 6' giant of a dad, and the lava of hot liquid showers anyone in a 3' radius. Drink too fast or when it's too hot, and a sputtering mouth full of caramel macchiato gives everyone a taste of your sweetness. Drinking can be dangerous.

Words, like coffee, can become messy when not held in a safe container, or when held too loosely. In this American world of freedom, right to speech, "I can say it if I think it," and "It's just my opinion, anyway," I often confuse liberty with needfulness. I want the world, ok, maybe not the whole world, but I have this desire at times to express my thoughts, opinions, beliefs, strategies, experiences, and whatever else has stumbled across my path to be part of your journey too. Some of it comes from my desire and passion to bring light into your world, educating you (as if you don't already know these things), perhaps bringing challenge, hope, and encouragement, and coming from a little bit of narcissism. The big, great big stopper, or lid on the cup, is when I stop to ask myself, "Is it necessary? Is it helpful?"

This has been on my mind the past few days as I finished listening to two books by an author, widely popular, influencing a million or so people, who is right smack dab in the middle of a crisis of faith, or dark night of the soul. I was overwhelmed with sadness in listening to this writer's story. I just want to go sit with this person and be a non-anxious presence, just hold the person's hand, and tell this author how much the writer is loved by so many. There are many things I want to say, but when someone is in the middle of the darkness, words fall like condensation from the cave ceiling, leaving one cold and shivering. I'd rather be a warm presence.

The struggle I'm having, and feeling a sense of conviction about, is the power of words. What if this author's words prevent others from seeking God? Or causes the reader to give up on the Church? Or on Christ, faith, or people? That frightens me, not so much for myself, but for those who are babes in their spiritual search and are so thirsty that they'll settle for that 5-cent coffee that's bitter and cold.

I don't begrudge this writer's plunge into the abyss. Most of us dive into that hole, or are thrown into it, at different points when life brings existential storms. St. John of the Cross wrote a treatise entitled, *Dark Night of the Soul*, "Into this dark night souls begin to enter when God draws them forth from the state of beginners – which is the state of those that meditate on the spiritual road – and begins to set them in the state of progressives – which is that of those who are already contemplatives – to the end that, after passing through it, they may arrive at the state of the perfect, which is that of the Divine union of the soul with God" (p. 15). He uses the rest of his manuscript to describe this state of testing. It's a movement from pablum as a babe in Christ to the testing and refining of one's faith. It comes in different forms for all us but it is necessary to deepen and strengthen our commitment to Christ.

The problem lies in the influence of another person's faith journey. I recall an adult who was agnostic. When I asked about how she came to that point, she said, "My pastor told me when I was teen that God didn't really exist, so it didn't matter what I believed. So, I stopped believing." I was furious upon hearing this. What gall. Talk about wrapping a chain around a baby's neck and throwing it off the cliff. Such inopportune words in the midst of great opportunity to influence. And yet, I am so guilty of this as well. I can recall times when I've spoken flippantly, not taking into account how what spills out of my mouth may deter someone else from seeking God's presence. My heart hurts knowing this, and I sit condemned, knowing that my verbiage now cannot absolve that sin.

Those who know me well know that I am no stranger to critical reflection, and the two people who read our book, *Discovery Teaching Like Jesus*, realize that I encourage questions, exploration of the unfathomable, and rebellion against the status quo. But, let me repeat, but only insomuch as that exploration leads one into a transformation of faith, and that deep diving moves one to ultimately become a change maker, bringing the light and life of the Gospel into the world. Otherwise, it's just an empty clanging bell, tolling a death march towards unevolved worship of self and vain philosophy.

I see you. I hear your cry. Sometimes we operate in systems that have difficulty allowing people to suffer and express their moments of doubts and confusion. That's when we need true community, a safe place, a container to privately describe the crack in our faith foundation, and loving people who will sit quietly with us, praying for the Holy Spirit to help us make our way through that. When we don't have those places or those people, we tend to make our outcries public.

I don't want to tell you what you can or cannot say. I refuse to play social media police or editor to your story. What I'm asking is that you bear responsibility for your words, just like I need to for my own. Find trusted people and let them witness your struggle with the angel. You may emerge with a limp like Jacob (Gen. 3:22-32), but that will serve as a reminder that you met God face to face, and you challenged him to bless you. Trust me, God will reveal God to you when you do that. We only have to remember Job, Noah, Jonah, should I name more? James reminds us, "A bit in the mouth of a horse controls the whole horse. A small rudder on a huge ship in the hands of a skilled captain sets a course in the face of the strongest winds. A word out of your mouth may seem of no account, but it can accomplish nearly anything – or destroy it" (3:3-5)!

Believe me, my mouth has got me in more trouble than I can ever make up for and has damaged a lot of relationships. My words have also brought light and life. That's where I want to keep it. Blessings, my friends, let's move beyond harming words.

Reflection

1. Think about the words you are speaking to yourself or others. In what ways do they hurt or harm you or others?

2. How can you begin to change those words?

3. What does it mean to be aware of your inner voice? How can you change your thoughts to speak God's truths?

_____

_____

_____

_____

_____

_____

_____

_____

BEYOND FAIRY TALES

Life isn't filled with magical moments,
and no one's life is perfect.
We all have our hurdles and we all have our battles.
But that's what makes life worth living.

Melisa Ergin

Writing a book on love made me notice couples. Have you ever seen such a mess? I'm a marriage therapist and so I have the honor to provide marital support to others. Folks, let me just say this. People have no idea what love is or how to find it. There is nothing that I have not seen or heard. I wish I could tell you some stories, but I cannot do that.

You see it, too, don't you? You wonder, why did those two get together? They're not a good fit. Or, "uh-oh," there's no way that pair will make it because they fight all the time. However, I've learned I'm not always the best predictor of who will last and who will not. But let's not be fooled. Just because two stay together does not mean they are living "happily ever after." I can guarantee you their car is in my parking lot. Sometimes it's the perfect pair who experience an imperfect relationship.

Movies, books, and other media lead us in believing we can have fairy tale lives. We just need a little pixie dust. The other day I asked a client what would make the session a success. The person replied, "If you fix my problem." Replying with a smile, I said, "Oh, I forgot my magic wand today." We both laughed.

Yet that's our expectation, isn't it? Life will be fair. Our prince will come. The princess is beautiful. We inherit a kingdom full of people who love us. Does that describe your life? Instead, we see injustice around us. Sometimes the handsome prince turns out to be a frog. The queen's attractiveness fades and where is that covey of worshipers, anyway? Life does not begin with once upon a time. Maybe that's not a bad thing.

I'm a realist, and often I disappoint my clients when I tell them what they face. I hate deflating their balloon of happy expectations. Yet I know if they keep trying to float the bubble high, they will face some unforeseeable force which will blow it somewhere they don't desire to be. Or some event will unexpectedly prick the bright ball and with one big POP!, their dream will disappear as quickly as it arrived.

Beginning with "Once upon a time" is good. But the in-between is vital to the relationship, and to life. It's the character-revealing, middle-of-the-story, grungy, stuck-in-the-ditch, facing dilemmas part of life that is endearing and enduring. Irreplaceable bonds happen during this time. It gives us the grit we need that strengthens our resolve and our relationships. Some days we don't like it and sometimes we just want to "hang it up." It's only in hindsight we realize how much we learn and grow from these no good, terrible days.

Right now is proof that life isn't a fairy tale. You're facing fearful enemies and fire-breathing dragons. Maybe I'm wrong. Maybe you're the person with the happily ever after, the eternal optimist who sees the good in everything. I envy you see life that way. I want to be like that. But I think some of us are the glass half-empty kind of people, always looking for a new way, a new job, a new person, an infusion of hope.

It sounds like I'm dismal, doesn't it? I'm not. As I think about it, I'm a happy person. I like getting dirt under my nails and dust in my hair. Those are the things that show me I've got what it takes to withstand any storm that comes my way. I'm a 2 Corinthians 4 kind of gal: "But we have this treasure in jars of clay to show that this all-surpassing power is from God and not from me. I am hard pressed on every side, but not crushed; perplexed, but not in despair; persecuted, but not abandoned; struck down, but not destroyed . . . life is at work in me" (v. 7 – 12). How about you? What describes you? I challenge you. Move beyond the fairy tale.

Reflection

1. What were your expectations of your life and family previously?

2. How were those realistic or not?

3. How are those changing now?

4. What expectations do you need to change for the future?

_____

_____

_____

_____

_____

BEYOND BITTERNESS

*As I walked out the door toward the gate
that would lead to my freedom,
I knew if I didn't leave my bitterness and hatred behind,
I'd still be in prison.*

Nelson Mandela

For some reason, I find myself thinking of bitterness. Recently I'm realizing that I'm moving beyond a sense of bitterness over some things that happened continuously throughout thirty years. In attending a workshop on forgiveness, I confirmed this. It's been a day at a time, but I no longer feel the pain of the hurt I endured. It's quite freeing. I'm just sad it took so long.

A few years ago, I painted a bitterroot flower when I painted all the state flowers. This gem is Montana's state flower and the root were a delicacy for Native Americans. Lewis Meriwether consumed it on his journey through the territory (National Park Service, 2018).

This made me remember a phrase I've heard about "eating bitter or bitterness." Apparently, it's a phrase used in China to teach children to accept whatever life brings, especially hardship and to learn how to dispel bitterness (Liljeblad, 2011).

Bitterness happens to many of us. I have fought this in my own life when I've been deeply wounded. Sometimes it's been a friend, a family member, a work colleague, or organization, even church. I've worked hard to let go of resentment.

But I'm also pretty sure that I'm not innocent in all this. I may have been the root of bitterness in someone else. For that I am truly sorry. That's when I want to practice steps 8 & 9 of the 12-step program: make a list of those I've offended and seek to make amends, except when it would bring more harm.

So here I am trying to hold contempt at bay and accepting my own shortcomings and bearing the weight of having caused harm to others. Well, I have absolutely no control over whether others will forgive me or not. But I can manage my thoughts and emotions about them, as I learned from Kelly McGonigal, at Stanford University, the practice of compassion in her book, The Science of

Compassion. Whenever bad thoughts arise about a person, place, or organization, I say, "Lord, may he/she/they experience your compassion today." Then for myself I whisper, "Lord, May I experience your compassion today." And then I practice kindness, tenderness, and forgiveness. How about you? How's your bitterness level?

Paul says, "Let all bitterness and wrath and anger and clamor and slander be put away from you, along with all malice. Be kind to one another, tenderhearted, forgiving one another, as God in Christ forgave you" (Ephesians 4:31-32, NIV). Easier said than done, right? So, how do we move beyond bitterness? Forgiveness. Practicing forgiveness every day. I tell my clients, "Forgiveness is not a feeling. It's a decision. It's a daily act, sometimes every day, for as long as it takes. It means saying, 'Dear person, organization, friend, spouse, whomever, I choose to forgive you today. Not because I feel it, not because you are or are not deserving, but because I love God and He forgave me.' I forgive you for hurting me." Then I do it again, and again, and again. Forgiveness untangles the roots - those bitter roots - and brings freedom to me. What do you need to do to move beyond bitterness?

Reflection

1. When you think about how this crisis has impacte you, what feelings of resentment or bitterness arise?

2. How does this keep you from being whole?

3. What steps do you need to take to let go of your bitterness?

BEYOND DISUNITY

Unity to be real must stand the severest strain without breaking.

Mahatma Gandhi

In preparation for a recent retreat, I spent time in prayer, reflection, and reading. The retreat, MOSAIC, a Montage Of Stories And InterConnection, was meant to help us notice the universality of what it means to be humans facing life's challenges, to discover the redemptive healing of God, and to use the transformative power of Christ to reach others who exist on the fringes, either by choice, circumstance, or prejudice. Thus, the vision statement for the retreat was "unity out of brokenness – until the margins become mainstream." The idea of a mosaic came to my mind when discussing the vision with the women's ministry leaders.

Mosaics are a beautiful piece of art that portray a unified picture or symbol, and yet composed of hundreds or thousands of pieces of glass, ceramic, or shells. It's incredible that a master designer can envision the whole and yet choose individual fragments and place them precisely where they need to be in the composition. My prayer is that those women, many like myself who feel isolated or distant from the corporate body, are pulled into the center of the action to be used by God.

It's about being one, isn't it? In John 17, Jesus says, "I'm praying not only for them but also for those who will believe in me because of them and their witness about me" (v. 20). Yes, that's the mission of the church – to develop Jesus followers who become difference makers for a world of people far from God. Oh, but wait a minute. How does that happen? What does it mean to be a Jesus follower?

I know many of us don't want to admit this – we're sinners – yep, every single one of us (Romans 3:10-12). Have you acknowledged that? It's the first step. Think about what that means. In some ways, we must return to Genesis 3 and the story of Adam and Eve. Living in a perfect paradise, given one command, and neither of them can keep that one rule. As a result, a fracture occurs – in their relationship, in the garden, in the world. The entire world suffers and is broken.

Whether we feel it or not, we are like cracked alabaster jars of clay leaking our contents wherever we go. It's why we labor so hard, why we struggle with self-identity, why we are unsuccessful in relationships, work, or in parenting. We simply cannot patch that container. We might as well try holding our finger in the dike just like the little Dutch boy, thinking he can prevent the onslaught of a watery demise. But that finger is getting tired, and no matter how hard we try, the fissure in the clay cannot be fixed. It is in recognizing our brokenness that we find the One who has the power to recreate our lives. Jesus aptly says, "You're blessed when you've lost it all. God's kingdom is there for the finding" (Luke 20). You see, it's in our poverty that we recognize our need for one who can mend us.

Upon being restored, we find our greatest joy, which excites us enough to proclaim, like John the Baptist, "There is one greater than me!" That's when we begin to make a difference. But is awareness and proclamation enough? Is that all it takes to become difference makers? Or do we need to go deeper?

Certainly, it wasn't enough for Jesus or the disciples. Otherwise, there was no need to do anything else. Yet, we find them, not only preaching and teaching, but developing workable plans to care for orphans and widows, and healing and caring. They speak to issues of justice and injustice, always pointing to Christ, but never stopping at "confess your sin, repent, accept Jesus, be baptized." They get down in the dirt and end up with criticism and persecution because a broken world only knows how to deal with the ugly, and not the glory of the redeemed. The Evil One creeps around whispering, "Surely you won't die. Surely, you're not broken. Maybe others are, but not you. You've done enough. Just relax. Volunteer a little with people you like." We could go on and on, couldn't we?

Jesus reiterated the mission for us from Isaiah. "The Spirit of God, the Master, is on me because God anointed me. He sent me to preach good news to the poor, heal the heartbroken, announce freedom to all captives, pardon all prisoners. God sent me to announce the year of his grace – a celebration of God's destruction of our enemies – and to comfort all who mourn" (Isaiah 61). My brokenness makes me focus on me and what I need and then separates me from others, except those with whom I'm comfortable. We may think it's about finding our "tribe" – those who meet our needs and we meet theirs, but maybe, perhaps, God means for us to go beyond and "enlarge our tents" so that our tribe just gets bigger.

I remember teaching a family therapy class and explaining how to do a genogram. It's basically a diagram of one's family tree. One student from Nigeria questioned me about this. Thinking it was a miscommunication issue, I tried to explain it in a different way. He shook his head and said, "No. You don't understand. My father is chief of our tribe. He has 167 wives and over 250 children." I replied, "Oh, that's a large piece of paper." It's a big tribe but everyone is cared for with the chief bearing primary responsibility. What would happen if I accepted more people in my tribe?

In her book, *Disunity in Christ*, Christena Cleveland talks about our tendency to encircle those with whom we have affinity.[40] We form our own little groups, and often end up defining ourselves as "right Christians" while others are "wrong Christians." Whether it's about political views, or theological beliefs, or socioeconomic status, we tend to silo ourselves into comfy buddies. The problem, she states, is this lack of diversity causes a narrowing view of what's right and wrong, ultimately producing disunity in our churches. We become separated into our groups. And in so doing, we filter who enters, who stays, and who leaves. You know what I'm talking about.

"Let's try to visit Resurrection Group today." Entering the room, we notice that we're not the right age, or wearing the same clothes, or talking about similar topics. While the crowd is welcoming, there's no invitation for coffee, or even to sit beside them in church. Perhaps we share a thought and are greeted with silence and furtive glances. If we're astute, we notice those who are "shunning" us. We are not welcome here and should we try again, likely we will be ignored at the next few visits. We do this all the time to one another. If you, or I, or someone doesn't fit the group norm, they will find subtle ways to distance us. If we think a person might be too "needy," or "commanding," or whatever we dislike, we will immediately judge this person as "not fitting." We are promoting disunity. Ouch, right?

But Jesus says, "When the world sees they [Christians] are one, they will see me" (John 17:21). Despite our preaching, our great testimonies, our volunteer work, are we working against God? Do non-believers see that we are one? Can they see the exquisite mosaic, or do they simply see broken fragments? How do we move beyond disunity? Cleveland says, "the cognitive processes that drive categorization are most powerful when they are hidden from sight. Once individuals become consciously aware of these processes . . . the processes begin to lose their power" [41]

Perhaps awareness is the beginning of being a difference maker. I'm becoming acutely aware of my own unfortunate dismissal of those who act and think differently. I feel a sense of shame, in a way, and wouldn't it be convenient for the Evil One to use that guilt to immobilize me? God's Spirit says, "Go beyond. Reach out. Keep pressing on. Hold your hand out. Open your heart." I pray we will be one so that the world may see Christ. What are you doing to go beyond disunity?

Reflection

1. How is this current situation providing opportunities for unity?

2. What have you done to bring people together in harmony?

3. How can you continue to seek unity in the future?

BEYOND BALANCE

You have to balance your passions, not your time.

Lisa Sugar

It never fails that I hear from other people, clients, friends, or church people that they're trying to find balance in their lives. They need work-life balance or church-life balance as if one side is holding them down like a bully on the playground. Of course, I've never heard anyone say they need more "work" or more "church" in that seesaw. As if they need more life. I don't even know what that means. Does it mean they need more time at home? More time with their spouse or children? More time to do chores? Or gardening? Or what exactly? And, it's usually in response to a request or an invitation to do something.

Perhaps it happens because people don't know how to say no. I was talking separately with a friend and client about this. When you don't want to do something, there are two ways to respond. First, just be silent. Nothing makes another person squirm more than silence and sometimes that's all that's needed to provide your response. You don't have to say yes to everything but don't make up an excuse or defend your answer or rationalize it. (I like directness – it's so much more honest). The second response is just as simple. Just say no (with a period). No explanation. Ok, if you want to be polite, smile and say, "No, but thanks for thinking of me," or "No, thanks for asking."

Yet so many people revert to this idea that they need balance. I want to point out the dichotomous logic of that statement. I'll readily admit sometimes I do too much to the detriment of my health and circadian rhythm. And when I do, I don't think as well, and I tend to get emotional and start crying easily. Those are sure signs that I need rest. But I don't think my life is "out of balance."

The things I choose to do, as well as my work, is my life. There's no separating all of that. And 95% of it brings me great pleasure. I cannot imagine not doing all I do. And why would I separate church as if it were not part of my life? I don't really see Jesus saying, "Peter, John, hey guys, I really can't go on that fishing trip today. I need to regain some work-life or ministry-life balance." Huh? And his job was 24-7.

It's important to point out people usually refer to this when they feel a sense of dissatisfaction with life. I truly believe we become unhappy about the balance because of several things: our expectations of either others or ourselves, when we confuse pleasure and satisfaction, or when we think something is competing with our life.[42] It's about a sense of well-being, those things that bring health and satisfaction.[43]

Think about how your expectations of yourself or of others get in the way of your fulfillment. While it saddens me that Stephen Hawking lost his way spiritually, he certainly had something important to say about demands in life. "My expectations were reduced to zero when I was 21. Everything since then has been a bonus." Lisa Kleypas, NY Times bestseller says, "You are your own worst enemy. If you can learn to stop expecting impossible perfection, in yourself and others, you may find the happiness that has always eluded you." And Proverbs says, "The hope of the righteous is gladness, but the expectation of the wicked perishes" (10:28). I have a difficult time learning to tamper my hopes of myself and others. Do you?

While those desires of myself are part of the problem, I also mistake pleasure with satisfaction. In the flow theory, it is precisely a demanding event or activity that meets our need and becomes satisfying. In our book, *Essential Drops for Living*, my New York, NY: sister and I speak of this. "Sometimes hours may pass until I realize how wonderful it was [the activity] and that I need to move on. During those times, the goals seem clear, and I'm able to accomplish the most difficult things like writing a musical, or a book, or complete a class."[44] It's what Mihály Csíkszentmihály calls "finding flow." He says, "Flow is being completely involved in an activity for its own sake."[45] That's satisfying but not necessarily pleasurable in the moment. It's often quite challenging.

Alas, we tend to think that work and life are competitors. Or that volunteerism or church activities are vying for our life. But work and life shouldn't be enemies – they go together.[46] And we flow in and out of them. That makes so much more sense than trying to find some ambiguous balance, which actually doesn't exist, and usually peeves someone in the process. You can't separate your life into little compartments. I don't clock in and out of my life. All of it is my life and I can welcome and love it all. That allows my creative self, my administrative self, my fun-loving and serious self to be fully integrated.

The scripture doesn't tell us to find work-life or church-life balance. Rather, it says, "With all this going for us, my dear, dear friends, stand your ground. And don't hold back. Throw yourselves into the work of the Master, confident that nothing you do for him is a waste of time or effort" (I Corinthians 15:58).

So, if you want to say no, just say no but don't confuse refusal to participate in something as a protective barrier. it's ok to rest at times; other times we will be busy. Chopping up your life into work – church – life does not insulate you from burnout. In fact, it probably makes you more susceptible to it. You have a unique opportunity to consider how to re-order your life at this time. Let's move beyond balance. Find your flow!

Reflection

1. What are your learning about your life right now?

2. Is God calling you to rest, to re-order your life for the future?

3. How can you make changes now that will carry into the future?

_____

_____

_____

_____

_____

_____

BEYOND IDENTITY

*Before I can live with other folks I've got to live with myself.
The one thing that doesn't abide by majority rule
is a person's conscience.*

Harper Lee

We talked about this earlier. Who are you? How is this situation changing you? These are questions included in my initial assessment of people who come for help. People's reactions to these two questions provide me with a lot of information about their psychological and spiritual health. Most people are rattled by the questions, feeling unsure of the first and uncomfortable with the second. Remember, they know they're being evaluated.

Some have no idea who they are beyond their current role at work or in family life. "I'm a CPA." "I'm a wife and mother."

"But who are you?" I ask again. It's the second time I ask they begin to squirm. Either they're uncertain of my motivation in another inquiry, have ambiguity of what it means, or sometimes, they simply don't know who they are beyond their ascribed position in life.

Eventually I feel bad enough to let them off the hook and so I ask, "Who do other people say that you are?" While that's still a little tricky, it seems easier for people to answer.

It's a lot easier than when I ask a person their strengths. Should they be honest? Is that bragging or prideful? Perhaps they don't know their own resources. It's far easier to focus on our limitations and weaknesses, isn't it?

What do those questions tell me? They speak to several things. First, is ego strength. I know, here I go using some fancy psychological term. It's about a human being's sense of self, ability to practice self-awareness, self-evaluation, and degree of resiliency.[47] In other words, it's about healthy self-esteem. How do you view yourself and when under pressure or stress or criticism, are you able to maintain that positive view? If a person in my office readily answers the question of who they are, including their strengths, it's a clue of good ego strength.

However, I also ask this question to determine a person's sense of reality. If you're sitting in my office and begin to tell me you're the Queen of England, then I'm pretty sure that we need to get you some extra help. If you tell me you invented the car, then we have further problems.

Hopefully neither of your answers involve those statements. If they do, I'll likely be recommending you visit with a psychiatrist to determine if you have a thought disorder such as present in schizophrenia or bipolar disorder.

Another reason for asking these questions is to determine your critical reflective skills. Are you able to answer these questions or think about them? Your response matters because I need to know how you think, how you process information, and what type of intervention might be appropriate for you. If you're a concrete person, I'm likely not going to give you further abstract questions or homework assignments which only frustrate both of us. However, if you answer these thoroughly, I will approach our sessions with more critical reflection.

How much you tell me also makes a difference. If you are unable to focus and change thoughts frequently as you answer these questions, then I will further investigate for other psychological diagnoses, perhaps ADHD. Upon asking these questions recently, a young woman took 15" to answer the questions, jumping thought trains frequently, and eventually making it back to the original question. She then looked at me and said, "I guess I should tell you I have ADHD." I smiled and said, "Thanks for letting me know." Some people never get back to the original question and that is good information for me as well. It's all part of my evaluation.

If you're uncertain or unable to answer the question, that may be telling me it's an area we need to work on. Perhaps you don't think highly of yourself or are overly critical. It may be that you've never explored who you are or where you need to be. It's quite fascinating how two simple questions provide such good information in an assessment.

But, does it matter what we think of ourselves? Or should we depend on what others say about us? From a psychological viewpoint, I'm reminded of Psychology 101 in college when I learned about the Johari window.

Picture a window with four panes of glass. This window is a view into yourself. One pane is open or clear. It is this part of you that is clearly known by others and yourself. For example, I'm a person who likes to write blogs. That's clear to both you and me.

The 2nd pane is a blind area, or something you may see about me that I do not see about myself. It may be that you see I'm forgetting information and I don't realize it. Once in a classroom, I was talking about a word on the board and a student pointed out to me that the word I was speaking of was a different word than written on the board. I turned to look. Ah, yes, the student was correct.

The third pane are the things I know about myself that you don't know about me. Those are the secrets of my life I keep from you. And the fourth pane are things about me that neither you nor I see, that are totally unknown.

In therapy, a counselor will focus on the 2nd and 3rd pane, trying to help clients to be more honest and transparent, believing that is in the best interest of the person. Occasionally, something in pane 4 is revealed. It can be a significant area of growth but also can be disturbing.

Back to my question. Does it matter what I think of myself? Or what others think of me beyond the psychological? That's a sticky wicket.

Maybe, maybe not. It's helpful but only as I hold those up to what God says about who I am. What I say, or others, can be used by the Enemy to beat me down. Or can add to a narcissistic view. My view may be inaccurate, or others may not see me as God does (which is often the case). If either prevents me from being close to God, or fulfilling my God-given purpose, then it's not helpful. Ultimately, what God thinks of me is what's most important.

Think of the Gospel story of Simon whose name became Peter. I picture him as a blustery, hyperactive, risk-taking kind of man who seems to put his foot in his mouth a lot. I have a sort of respect and sadness for him. He has a tendency for impulsiveness, almost getting himself drowned trying to walk on water, or getting caught in a lie when he denies Christ, and yet becoming the rock upon which God builds the Church. A crowning moment for Peter is when Jesus poses the question I ask, but he tricks Peter by first asking who men think Jesus is.

Here's the passage in Matthew 16:13 – 20. When Jesus arrived in the villages of Caesarea Philippi, he asked his disciples, "What are people saying about who the Son of Man is?" They replied, "Some think he is John the Baptizer, some say Elijah, some Jeremiah or one of the other prophets." He pressed them, "And how about you? Who do you say I am?" Simon Peter said, "You're the Christ, the Messiah, the Son of the living God." Jesus came back, "God bless you, Simon, son of Jonah!" You didn't get that answer out of books or from teachers. My Father in heaven, God himself, let you in on this secret of who I really am. And now I'm going to tell you who you are, really are. You are Peter, a rock. This is the rock on which I will put together my church, a church so expansive with energy that not even the gates of hell will be able to keep it out.

Jesus moves from asking about what others say about him, to what Peter believes about him, and then proclaims Peter's identity. It is Peter's recognition of Christ that grants him a new persona, one that is kingdom-driven and glory-bound.

This leads me to move beyond what I think of myself or what others think of me to answer what I believe about Christ. Who do

I say Christ is and what does God say back to me about who I am? Am I a rock? Can the church be built upon what I say of Christ? Today, that question is challenging me to move beyond what I say or what others say. How about you? What do you need to do move beyond earthly identity?

Reflection

1. How is this event changing who you are?

2. What have you learned about yourself?

3. How does God want to use you in the future?

_____

_____

_____

_____

_____

_____

BEYOND EASTER

Do not abandon yourselves to despair.
We are the Easter people and hallelujah is our song.

Pope John Paul II

It's hard to believe it's Easter week. With the topsy-turvy world we're living in during this pandemic, and the accompanying social isolation, signs of Easter are rare. They actually seem out of place as I see ads for eggs, baskets, and clothing. I think I've worn the five same shirts and pants on each day for the past five weeks. Suddenly, the need for any of these seems trivial.

I heard Easter was cancelled. Of course, it wasn't but certainly attending a live service is out of the question. We're constrained to worship from our homes. Interesting, isn't it? Doesn't this place us right back to the first century? Perhaps, we'll have a bit more understanding of what the first Christians faced as they had to meet in homes, albeit we are sequestered and connecting wirelessly.

This change in holiday plans leaves me wonting and wanting. I miss the past experiences of Resurrection day where we arose early to attend sunrise service, attended the church pancake breakfast, and joined the choir in full regalia to sing "Christ, the Lord, is Risen Today!" This current situation leaves me wanting more – of people, of myself, and of God. I know it is my longing for God that will resurrect me during this season of death to life as we know it.

The Psalmist declares, "My soul is crushed with longing after your ordinances at all times" (Ps. 119:20). You see, somehow communion at home is not the same when it's done with others. Worshiping is different. There is a synergy absent. And baptisms done at 6 feet of difference is quite a challenge. I'm famished for connection with people in a room together. I miss the warmth, the vibes, the expression of affect that cannot be gained through technology.

We are in a time of famine, my friends. It may last a few weeks or a few months. Think about what you crave now. Do you miss your companions? Your favorite restaurants? Your routine? What are you hungry for?

While I'm not a touching person, I miss touch. I'm reminded of Harlow's classic experiments with monkeys that demonstrated the need for touch. In the 1960s, Harlow and other psychologists were determined to prove the importance of attachment to maternal beings. Infant monkeys were divided into groups. One group was provided with a surrogate mother made of cloth, and the other group a wire mother with a milk bottle. The monkeys would go to the wire mother for food but spent more time with the cloth mother. When frightened, they would run to the cloth mother.[48] The monkeys needed and wanted the experience of soft touch. One of the symptoms of reactive attachment disorder the avoidance of eye contact and physical touch.[49] My fear as we continue to dive deeper into social distancing is that we experience diminishing experiences of touch and comfort.

While families are able to provide that, in most cases, what about those who live alone or those who live in abusive or neglectful homes? While we are able to read, watch, and listen to God's words through others, we are missing that real, face-to-face interaction that stirs us deeply and spurs us to good works. Amos 8:11 says, "'Behold, days are coming,' declares the Lord God, 'When I will send a famine on the land, not a famine for bread or a thirst for water, but rather for hearing the words of the Lord.'"

There's only so much alone time that works for me and I'm an introvert! I can't imagine the difficulty all the extroverts may be having. That relates to our worship of God. With those familiar with the Myers-Briggs Personality Types, the spiritual yearnings of these types are important.

Extraversion or introversion is the way in which one gains energy. Thus, extroverts are energized through contact with people or through engaging in activities while introverts are energized from ideas, thoughts, and reflection. In the second realm of sensing or intuition, those who are sensors pay attention to information they receive from their five senses while intuitives pay attention to their sixth sense. When making decisions, thinkers use logic, cause and effect reasoning, while feeling types consider how decisions impact others. Lastly, people who prefer an orderly way of living are known as judging types while perceivers prefer spontaneity.[50] Now, think about how each experience God and how the current dilemma impacts all of that.

If extraverts need people to gain energy such as the live worship experience and serving opportunities, and that's how they find God, then how can they grow spiritually without those opportunities? And if introverts are dependent upon intuition, and thus the unstated and emotional energy of a group, and make decisions based upon the overall impact, how can they grow spiritually in the absence of those?

Pastor Deron Spoo of First Baptist Church, Tulsa, expresses it this way. "Whether by the choice of another or by circumstances beyond control, we will all face abandonment at some point in life. If we have used people to avoid God, when the people in our life are suddenly stripped away from us, we then realize we have no one from which to draw strength."[51] It is at this point that abandonment can draw people into closer intimacy with God as well as a deeper dependency.

We have a rare opportunity that most have never faced and will never face again. It's a chance to learn a lesson that moves us beyond Easter. You see, Christianity didn't end at Easter. It's a glorious celebration of Christ's sacrifice and redemption but it's not the end of the story. Just as Christ's story moved beyond the four gospels into Acts and all the mission experiences of Paul, Barnabas, Timothy, and John, and all of the first century Christians, so this is a calling for us to move beyond the Easter story.

When I accepted Christ and was baptized, I celebrated the death and resurrection of my Savior, and of my nature. But that wasn't enough. God called me to move beyond to become a disciple, a follower, and to become a difference maker in the world. He called me to be a pastor's wife, to be a counselor, and now to be a voice crying in the wilderness. "Make way for the Lord!"

This year we will forego the physical gathering to celebrate our Lord. But God is still at work, bringing redemption to all. Perhaps God's calling in this current catastrophe is a death to our former lives or the parts that were not working or honoring God. It's an invitation to experience a resurrection of a new life with different priorities. Finally, it's a message to move beyond normal and come a communal declaration, "World, everyone, all people.

Make way for the Lord!" Join me. What is God calling you to do beyond Easter? What is God calling you to do beyond this pandemonium?

Reflection

1. How will your life change now?

2. What do you need to do to be a difference maker in the world?

3. How will God use you in the future?

_____

_____

_____

_____

_____

_____

BIBLIOGRAPHY

Allan, D.G. (2017, Apr 28). Good and bad, it's all the same: A Taoist parable to live by.

Amatenstein, (2019, Nov 15). Not so social media: How social media increases loneliness. *PsyCom*.

"An introduction to the Achiever® CliftonStrengths theme." (2020). Gallup, Inc.

Beersma, B., & van Kleef, G.A. (2012). Why people gossip: An empirical analysis of social motives, antecedents, and consequences. *Journal of Applied Social Psychology, 42*(11), 2640-2670.

Boerner, K., Stroebe, M., Schut, H., & Wortman, C. B. (2016). Grief and bereavement: Theoretical perspectives. *Encyclopedia of Geropsychology*.

Boyce, B. (Ed.). (2011). *The mindfulness revolution*. Boston, MA: Shambhala Publications, Inc.

Clarke, M. A. (2003). Abiding loneliness: An existential

perspective on loneliness.

Cleveland, C. (2013). *Disunity in Christ: Uncovering the hidden forces that keep us apart.* Downers Grove, IL: IVP.

Cleveland Clinic. (2020). Reactive attachment disorder. What is reactive attachment disorder (RAD)?

Csíkszentmihály, M. (1990). *Flow: The psychology of optimal experience.* New York, NY: HarperCollins.

Dawson, R. (2015). Is religion good for your mental health? *The Way, 57*(1), 45-50.

Dein, S. (2010, Jan 10). Religion, spirituality, and mental health. *Psychiatric Times, 27*(1).

Foster, E. K. (2004). Research on gossip: Taxonomy, methods, and future directions. *Review of General Psychology, 8,* 78-99.

Gruebner, O., Rapp, M.A., Adli, M., Kluge, U., Galea, S., & Heinz, A. (2017, Feb). Cities and mental health. *Deutsches Arzteblatt International, 114*(8), 121 – 127.

Harlow, H.F., Dodsworth, R.O., & Harlow, M.K. (1965). Total

social isoltation in monkeys. *Proceedings of the National Academy of Sciences of the United States of America.*

Hirsh, S.K., & Kise, J.A.G. (2006). *SoulTypes: Matching your personality and spiritual path.* Minneapolis, MN: Augsburg Books.

Hoppe, K., & Bynum, C. (2019). *Essential drops for living.* Broken Arrow, OK: Author.

Ilies, R., Wagner, D., Wilson, K., Ceja, L., Johnson, M., DeRue, S., & Ilgen, D. (2017). Flow at work and basic psychological needs: Effects on well-being. *Applied Psychology: An International Review, 66*(1), 3-24.

Kelly, M. (2014). *Off balance: Getting beyond the work-life balance myth to personal and professional satisfaction.* New York, NY: Avery.

Koenig, H.G., McCullough, M.E., & Larson, D.B. (2001). *Handbook of religion and health.* Oxford, UK: Oxford University.

LePan, N. (2020, Mar 14). Visualizing the history of pandemics.

Visual Capitalist.

Litman, J.A., & Pezzo, M.V. (2005). Individual differences in attitudes towards gossip. *Personality and Individual Differences, 38*, 963-980.

Newburg, A. (2014). The neuroscientific study of spiritual practices. *Frontiers in Psychology, 5*, art. 215, 1-6.

Ngnoumen, C.T., & Langer, E. J. (2016). Mindfulness: The essence of well-being and happiness (ch. 6). In I. Ivtzan & T. Lomas (Eds.), *Mindfulness in positive psychology.* New York, NY: Routledge.

Nouwen, H.J.M. (1972). *The wounded healer.* Garden City, NY: Image Books.

Nouwen, H. (2009). *Our greatest gift: A meditation on dying and caring.* New York, NY: HarperCollins.

Over, H., & Cook, R. (2018, Jan). Where do spontaneous first impressions of faces come from? *Cognition, 170.*

Primack, B. A., Shensa, A., Sidani, J. E., Whaite, E. O., Lin, L., . . . & Miller, E. (2017), Mar 6). Social media use and perceived social isolation among young adults in the U. S. *American Journal of Preventive Medicine, 53*(1).

Reeves, R., Beazley, A., & Adams, C. (2011, Jun). Religion and spirituality: Can it adversely affect mental health treatment? *Journal of Psychosocial Nursing & Mental Health Services, 49*(6), 6-7.

Reis, H., Wheeler, L., Spiegel, N., Kernis, M., Nezlek, J., & Perri, M. (1982). Physical attractiveness in social interaction: Why does appearance affect social experience? *Journal of Personality and Social Psychology, 43*(5), 979-996.

Robbins, M.L., & Karan, A. (2019, May 2). Who gossips and how in everyday life? *Social Psychological and Personality Science.*

Singer, C. (2018, Spr). Health effects of social isolation and loneliness. *Journal of Aging Life Care, 28*(1), 4-8.

Smith, J.H. (2011). Word of the day: Harbinger.

Spoo, D. (2020). *The Bible in 10 words.* New York, NY: Worthy.

Staats, C., Capatosto, K., Tenney, L., & Mamo, S. (2017). State of the science: Implicit bias review.

Staik, A. (2016, Aug). Mirror neurons: How our ability to connect with others makes us caring, moral by nature. *Neuroscience & Relationships.*

Stalk, A. (2017, Aug 5). Ego versus ego-strength: The characteristics of a healthy ego and why it's essential to your happiness.

Stroebe, M., Schut, H., & Boerner, K. (2017). Cautioning healthcare professionals: Bereaved persons are misguided through the stages of grief. *OMEGA – Journal of Death and Dying, 74*(4), 455-475.

Todorov A., Said, C., & Verosky, S. (2012). Personality impressions from facial appearances. In G. Rhodes, A. Calder, M. Johnson, & J. V. Haxby, *Oxford handbook of face perception.*

Van Nuys, D. (n.d.). An interview with George Bonanno, Ph.D., on bereavement.

Viorst, J. (2012). *Alexander and the terrible, horrible, no good, very bad day.* New York, NY: Simon & Schuster.

Windsteiger, L. (2017, Jun 27). How our narrowing social circles create a more unequal world.

Wolfe, T. (1930). *God's lonely man.*

Xu, Z., Muller, M., Heekeren, K., Theodoridou, A., Metzler, S., . . . & Rusch, N. (2016). Pathways between stigma and suicidal ideation among people at risk of psychosis. *Schizophrenia Research, 172*(1-3), 184-188.

ABOUT THE AUTHOR

Kathy Hoppe is a licensed marital and family therapist, adjunct faculty member, minister, and conference leader. She has worked in the fields of mental health and ministry in private, group, hospital, medical centers, hospices, and employee assistance programs. She has taught undergraduate and graduate courses at seven universities. She has a Doctor of Ministry from Oral Roberts University, a Master of Divinity from Golden Gate Baptist Theological Seminary, a Master of Science in general psychology from Grand Canyon University, and a Bachelor of Arts in psychology from the University of North Texas. Additionally, she is a certified compassion fatigue specialist and has a certificate in online teaching and learning and a postgraduate certificate in marriage and family therapy approved by the Commission on Marriage and Family Therapy Education (COAMFTE).

ENDNOTES

[1] LePan, N. (2020, Mar 14). Visualizing the history of pandemics. *Visual Capitalist.*

[2] Primack, B. A., Shensa, A., Sidani, J. E., Whaite, E. O., Lin, L., . . . & Miller, E. (2017), Mar 6). Social media use and perceived social isolation among young adults in the U. S. *American Journal of Preventive Medicine, 53*(1).

[3] Amatenstein, (2019, Nov 15). Not so social media: How social media increases loneliness. *PsyCom.*

[4] Singer, C. (2018, Spr). Health effects of social isolation and loneliness. *Journal of Aging Life Care, 28*(1), 4-8.

[5] Xu, Z., Muller, M., Heekeren, K., Theodoridou, A., Metzler, S., . . . & Rusch, N. (2016). Pathways between stigma and suicidal ideation among people at risk of psychosis. *Schizophrenia Research, 172*(1-3), 184-188.

[6] Gruebner, O., Rapp, M.A., Adli, M., Kluge, U., Galea, S., & Heinz, A. (2017, Feb). Cities and mental health. *Deutsches Arzteblatt International, 114*(8), 121 – 127.

[7] Staik, A. (2016, Aug). Mirror neurons: How our ability to connect with others makes us caring, moral by nature. *Neuroscience & Relationships.*

[8] Wolfe, T. (1930). *God's lonely man.*

[9] Spoo, D. (2020). *The Bible in 10 words.* New York, NY: Worthy.

[10] "An introduction to the Achiever® CliftonStrengths theme."

[11] Clarke, M. A. (2003). Abiding loneliness: An existential perspective on loneliness.

[12] Reis, H., Wheeler, L., Spiegel, N., Kernis, M., Nezlek, J., & Perri, M. (1982). Physical attractiveness in social interaction:

Why does appearance affect social experience? *Journal of Personality and Social Psychology, 43*(5), 979-996.

[13] Todorov A., Said, C., & Verosky, S. (2012). Personality impressions from facial appearances. In G. Rhodes, A. Calder, M. Johnson, & J. V. Haxby, *Oxford handbook of face perception.*

[14] Over, H., & Cook, R. (2018, Jan). Where do spontaneous first impressions of faces come from? *Cognition, 170.*

[15] Windsteiger, L. (2017, Jun 27). How our narrowing social circles create a more unequal world.

[16] Staats, C., Capatosto, K., Tenney, L., & Mamo, S. (2017). State of the science: Implicit bias review.

[17] Nouwen, H.J.M. (1972). *The wounded healer.* Garden City, NY: Image Books.

[18] Van Nuys, D. (n.d.). An interview with George Bonanno, Ph.D., on bereavement.

[19] Stroebe, M., Schut, H., & Boerner, K. (2017). Cautioning healthcare professionals: Bereaved persons are misguided through the stages of grief. *OMEGA – Journal of Death and Dying, 74*(4), 455-475.

[20] Boerner, K., Stroebe, M., Schut, H., & Wortman, C. B. (2016). Grief and bereavement: Theoretical perspectives. *Encyclopedia of Geropsychology.*

[21] Raghunathan, R. (2016). *If you're so smart, why aren't you happy?* New York, NY: Portfolio/Penguin.

[22] Raghunathan, R.

[23] Ngnoumen, C.T., & Langer, E. J. (2016). Mindfulness: The essence of well-being and happiness (ch. 6). In I. Ivtzan & T. Lomas (Eds.), *Mindfulness in positive psychology.* New York, NY: Routledge.

[24] Boyce, B. (Ed.). (2011). *The mindfulness revolution.* Boston, MA: Shambhala Publications, Inc.

[25] Reeves, R., Beazley, A., & Adams, C. (2011, Jun).

Religion and spirituality: Can it adversely affect mental health treatment? *Journal of Psychosocial Nursing & Mental Health Services, 49*(6), 6-7.

[26] Newburg, A. (2014). The neuroscientific study of spiritual practices. *Frontiers in Psychology, 5*, art. 215, 1-6.

[27] Dawson, R. (2015). Is religion good for your mental health? *The Way, 57*(1), 45-50.

[28] Koenig, H.G., McCullough, M.E., & Larson, D.B. (2001). *Handbook of religion and health.* Oxford, UK: Oxford University.

[29] Dein, S. (2010, Jan 10). Religion, spirituality, and mental health. *Psychiatric Times, 27*(1).

[30] Koenig, et al. (2001).

[31] Foster, E. K. (2004). Research on gossip: Taxonomy, methods, and future directions. *Review of General Psychology, 8*, 78-99.

[32] Litman, J.A., & Pezzo, M.V. (2005). Individual differences in attitudes towards gossip. *Personality and Individual Differences, 38*, 963-980.

[33] Robbins, M.L., & Karan, A. (2019, May 2). Who gossips and how in everyday life? *Social Psychological and Personality Science.*

[34] Robbins & Karan.

[35] Beersma, B., & van Kleef, G.A. (2012). Why people gossip: An empirical analysis of social motives, antecedents, and consequences. *Journal of Applied Social Psychology, 42*(11), 2640-2670.

[36] Smith, J.H. (2011). Word of the day: Harbinger.

[37] Allan, D.G. (2017, Apr 28). Good and bad, it's all the same: A Taoist parable to live by.

[38] Viorst, J. (2012). *Alexander and the terrible, horrible, no good, very bad day.* New York, NY: Simon & Schuster.

[39] Nouwen, H. (2009). *Our greatest gift: A meditation on*

dying and caring. New York, NY: HarperCollins.

[40] Cleveland, C. (2013). *Disunity in Christ: Uncovering the hidden forces that keep us apart.* Downers Grove, IL: IVP.

[41] Cleveland, C.

[42] Kelly, M. (2014). *Off balance: Getting beyond the work-life balance myth to personal and professional satisfaction.* New York, NY: Avery.

[43] Ilies, R., Wagner, D., Wilson, K., Ceja, L., Johnson, M., DeRue, S., & Ilgen, D. (2017). Flow at work and basic psychological needs: Effects on well-being. *Applied Psychology: An International Review, 66*(1), 3-24.

[44] Hoppe, K., & Bynum, C. (2019). *Essential drops for living.* Broken Arrow, OK: Author.

[45] Csíkszentmihály, M. (1990). *Flow: The psychology of optimal experience.* New York, NY: HarperCollins.

[46] Ilies, et al.

[47] Stalk, A. (2017, Aug 5). Ego versus ego-strength: The characteristics of a healthy ego and why it's essential to your happiness.

[48] Harlow, H.F., Dodsworth, R.O., & Harlow, M.K. (1965). Total social isoltation in monkeys. *Proceedings of the National Academy of Sciences of the United States of America.*

[49] Cleveland Clinic. (2020). Reactive attachment disorder. What is reactive attachment disorder (RAD)?

[50] Hirsh, S.K., & Kise, J.A.G. (2006). *SoulTypes: Matching your personality and spiritual path.* Minneapolis, MN: Augsburg Books.

[51] Spoo, D. (2020). *The Bible in 10 words.* New York, NY: Worthy.